AFGHANISTAN: HONORING THE HEROES OF EXTORTION 17

HEARING

BEFORE THE

SUBCOMMITTEE ON NATIONAL SECURITY

OF THE

COMMITTEE ON OVERSIGHT AND GOVERNMENT REFORM

HOUSE OF REPRESENTATIVES

ONE HUNDRED THIRTEENTH CONGRESS

SECOND SESSION

FEBRUARY 27, 2014

Serial No. 113–98

Printed for the use of the Committee on Oversight and Government Reform

Available via the World Wide Web: http://www.fdsys.gov
http://www.house.gov/reform

U.S. GOVERNMENT PRINTING OFFICE

87–499 PDF   WASHINGTON : 2014

For sale by the Superintendent of Documents, U.S. Government Printing Office
Internet: bookstore.gpo.gov   Phone: toll free (866) 512–1800; DC area (202) 512–1800
Fax: (202) 512–2104   Mail: Stop IDCC, Washington, DC 20402–0001

(II)

CONTENTS

AFGHANISTAN: HONORING THE HEROES OF EXTORTION 17

Thursday, February 27, 2014

House of Representatives,
Subcommittee on National Security,
Committee on Oversight and Government Reform,
Washington, D.C.

The subcommittee met, pursuant to call, at 10:04 a.m., in Room 2154, Rayburn House Office Building, Hon. Jason Chaffetz [chairman of the subcommittee] presiding.

Present: Representatives Chaffetz, Lummis, Mica, Duncan, Amash, Woodall, Tierney, Maloney, Lynch, Speier, Kelly, Welch, and Grisham.

Also Present: Representatives Rigell and Fortenberry.

Staff Present: Brien A. Beattie, Professional Staff Member; Adam P. Fromm, Director of Member Services and Committee Operations; Linda Good, Chief Clerk; Frederick Hill, Director of Communications and Senior Policy Advisor; Mitchell S. Kominsky, Counsel; Jim Lewis, Senior Policy Advisor; John Ohly, Professional Staff Member; Laura Rush, Deputy Chief Clerk; Sarah Vance, Assistant Clerk; Sang H. Yi, Professional Staff Member; Jaron Bourke, Minority Director of Administration; Devon Hill, Minority Research Assistant; Jennifer Hoffman, Minority Press Secretary; Peter Kenny, Minority Counsel; Chris Knauer, Minority Senior Investigator; Julia Krieger, Minority New Media Press Secretary; Elisa LaNier, Minority Deputy Clerk; Juan McCullum, Minority Clerk; and Dave Rapallo, Minority Staff Director.

Mr. CHAFFETZ. Committee will come to order. Thank you all for being here. I—this hearing, Afghanistan, Honoring the Heroes of Extortion 17, has been extraordinarily difficult to organize this hearing, because it's proved nearly impossible to effectively solicit and subsequently meet the needs and wishes of every family member and loved one that was onboard Extortion 17.

I want to assure the families that this committee has questioned the Department of Defense officials on the full spectrum of the mission, to include extremely sensitive and highly classified information, in an effort to fully understand the events pertaining to the tragedy that unfolded that day. We have tried our best to treat all the families' interests equally, knowing that there's a wide range of spectrum and perspectives, given the sheer number of people and families that are engaged in this.

Two of these—two of our—America's best happen to be from my congressional district in Utah. And a number of members obviously care deeply about this issue. You're going to see members coming

(1)

and going in this hearing. We have lots of different things happening here in Congress at the same time.

Some families may claim we have not done enough by not allowing classified or highly graphic information to be discussed today and others may claim that any discussion about Extortion 17 is counterproductive and opens old wounds. If I did not believe that the majority of the families wanted a forum like this to exist, we would not be conducting this hearing. It is extremely sensitive. There are things that we cannot and will not be discussing in this hearing, given the classified nature. I hope people will understand that. That's the way the United States of America operates. And our first and foremost concern is to make sure that we protect the ongoing lives and operations of the United States military. But I will say that the United States is different than the rest of the world. We are open, we are transparent, we are self-critical, and we do so in the spirit of making things better.

I'd also—so today as we start this, I'd like to welcome Ranking Member Tierney of the subcommittee, particularly Congressman Lynch, who's shown a great deal of interest in this. I want to welcome Mr. Rigell, who's spent a lot of time on this. Although not a member of this committee, I appreciate his presence here today.

On August 6th of 2011, Taliban insurgents killed 30 American servicemen, including 17 Navy SEALs, making it the largest single day loss of life in naval special warfare history and the largest single day loss of life during the war in Afghanistan. The events that unfolded that night are commonly referred to as Extortion 17, which is the call sign for the helicopter transporting the special operations personnel.

We are here today at the request of many of the families of the fallen heroes aboard Extortion 17 to obtain answers to their questions where answers can be found. This hearing also serves to honor the 30 American servicemen aboard Extortion 17 and their families. I've traveled to Afghanistan numerous times, visited with the servicemen and women there, and have nothing but the greatest respect and admiration that are serving our country.

Over the course of many months, the committee has had an open and ongoing dialogue with many of the families and servicemen, families of the servicemen aboard Extortion 17. In an effort to find answers to many of the outstanding questions regarding Extortion 17, some concerning the operation, others regarding postmortem events, we have welcomed the families to communicate their thoughts and concerns with the committee.

In addition to attending a funeral of one of the servicemen aboard Extortion 17, I personally met with some of the families of the 30 servicemen to hear their concerns and listen carefully to what questions they had about the tragic event.

I offer my deepest condolences to all the families who've lost a loved one as a result of this incredibly tragic event. My heart also goes out to the bigger, broader military family and community, because I know how much they care about their colleagues and friends and people that they serve with.

It is important as a Nation we not forget the service of all the men and women who serve this country. They've served us in the past, they're serving us now, and they will serve us in the future.

In advance of this hearing, the committee staff has invited and encouraged families to submit written testimony for the record and to pass on some of their questions that may be directed to the Department of Defense by Members of Congress. There is an order and a process to this, which I'm proud to help facilitate.

Because the committee takes the concerns of families with great sincerity, for more than 8 months we have been reviewing the facts surrounding Extortion 17. The committee has performed an extensive review of almost 2,000 pages of unclassified material related to Extortion 17, the committee has also met with independent sources with direct and indirect knowledge of the facts surrounding Extortion 17.

To address some of the unanswered questions, the committee received briefings, classified and unclassified, on the operational component leading up to the loss of the 30 servicemen and eight Afghan nationals, and on the postmortem handling of the 30 American servicemen on Extortion 17.

I'd like to take a moment to thank the Department of Defense for their cooperation with the subcommittee in providing answers to many of the questions I have asked and others have asked of the Department. The facts surrounding Extortion 17 are terribly heartbreaking, and we appreciate the candor and willingness to answer difficult questions from both sides of the aisle. The committee has reviewed these facts in a bipartisan way, we have had open, transparent dialogue with our colleagues on both sides of the aisle.

Today the committee will be specifically looking into whether the remains of U.S. personnel were treated with the proper respect they deserve, and whether Department of Defense procedures were followed and sufficient. I strongly believe that every fallen hero deserves to be treated with the proper amount of dignity and respect. If there are concerns calling into question the Department policies, we are here today to have productive discussion on how we can ensure the proper treatment of the remains of servicemen.

I'd like to emphasize, it is the intent of the subcommittee to obtain all the available information about the events following the crash of Extortion 17, dispel potential myths, and to learn from the event so we can assure that proper reforms are implemented.

I want to take a moment to recognize the dedication of our loyal servicemen to this country in maintaining the security and bedrock of our principles. In this vein, I'm greatly saddened that 1,795 U.S. military personnel have given their lives to serve in Afghanistan since September 11th, 2001, and 19,665 have been wounded in action during that same time frame. We must pay respect to those men and women and their families and thank them for their service. I personally believe as a community, as a Nation, we can do more to help and support and recognize and honor them.

At that same time, I want to commend the witnesses, three of which are dressed in uniform and two retired officers for their service to this country and thank them for appearing before this subcommittee on a very difficult topic. Their heart's in the right place, having met with them and chatted with them. They serve our Nation. We honor them and we thank you for what it—in attending what is obviously a very difficult topic, but we appreciate your service and we thank you for being here today.

With that, I'd now like to recognize the distinguished Ranking Member, the gentlemen from Massachusetts, Mr. Tierney, for his opening statement.

Mr. TIERNEY. Thank you, Mr. Chairman. Before we begin today, I think it's extremely important that we honor the lives of all of our fallen heroes for the untold contributions that they've made to the service of this country and to the families who mourn their losses. We need to remember that not only did we lose 30 great warriors that night in the Afghan battlefield, but the burden is now carried by the families who lost sons and fathers, brothers and husbands.

I'd also like to acknowledge that some of the families are here with us today. For you and the other families who couldn't attend today's proceedings, I want to express my profound gratitude for your sons' service and also express my condolences for your loss.

Mr. Chairman, I understand that there are some out there who strongly believe this hearing is necessary, and there are other families and their representatives who have contacted the subcommittee and expressed great concern about today's hearing. They've asked for privacy and they seek closure. So I realize that some have more questions about what happened; we should acknowledge that not all of the families affected with this tragedy support these proceedings. And I have confidence, Mr. Chairman, that you will make all efforts to conduct today's discussion with both dignity and fairness.

I think it's also important to acknowledge that earlier this week, senior officials from the Pentagon provided an extensive briefing to members and staff, where many questions were asked and answered about the topics that we may not be able to discuss at today's hearing. We also received an unclassified briefing last week on some of the post operations concerns that you do intend to discuss today. Pentagon officials provided answers to many questions, and I look forward to their testimony today, which I hope may provide some answers to those that are still seeking them.

Mr. Chairman, I would also like to acknowledge the distinguished men and women on today's panel. These officials also serve their country. Some have even served in harm's way and others served as one of the final caretakers of our fallen heroes. During the briefings last week, we heard from these officials just how humbling their work truly is, and it is not made it any easier by the fact that the fallen heroes are also their comrades.

Finally, Mr. Chairman, I want to conclude by noting that to date, we have lost 2,175 great Americans during the war in Afghanistan and tens of thousands and others who have been wounded and severely debilitated.

While we are here today to discuss the events surrounding the tragic deaths of 30 brave Americans, let's also take the opportunity to acknowledge the thousands of men and women who have sacrificed and paid the ultimate price in their service to this country. Thank you, Mr. Chairman.

Mr. MICA. Mr. Chairman, I have a unanimous consent request. I would request, Mr. Chairman, that after your remarks and the remarks of the ranking member, that we insert in the record of this hearing at this point the names of those individuals, servicemen who lost their life in the C–47 Chinook helicopter disaster. And I would ask that that be printed immediately after your remarks.

Mr. CHAFFETZ. Without objection, so ordered.

I'd like to also thank again the members of our—of our subcommittee for attending today. I'd also like to recognize Mr. Fortenberry from Nebraska, who's been very active and involved and engaged in this issue, and I appreciate his presence here today.

I would also remind members that they may have 7 days to submit opening statements for the record. That would be all members, even those that do not serve here on our committee.

It's now, at this point, I'd like to recognize our panel. And we have members representing the Pentagon, and we have Mr. Garry P. Reid, who's the Principal Deputy Assistant Secretary of the Defense For Special Operations and Low Intensity Conflict at the United States Department of Defense; Ms. Deborah Skillman, is the director of Casualty and Mortuary Affairs at the United States Department of Defense; we have Colonel John Devillier. Devillier? Devillier—my apologies—is the Commander of Air Force Mortuary Affairs Operations at the United States Department of Defense; Colonel Kerk Brown is the director of Army Casualty and Mortuary Affairs—Mortuary Affairs Operations Center at the United States Department of Defense. And we have Commander Aaron Brodsky who is the director of Navy Casualty Services at the United States Department of Defense.

Pursuant to committee rules, all witnesses will be sworn before they testify. If you'd please rise and raise your right hands. Do you solemnly swear or affirm that the testimony you're about to give will be the truth, the whole truth and nothing but the truth? Thank you. You may be seated. Let the record reflect that the witnesses all answered in the affirmative.

As we have discussed with the Department of Defense, I want our audience, and particularly the families, to know that there are some limitations in things that we can discuss. As I've mentioned, there are certain classified information, certain things about the actual operation itself that we cannot and will not in a non-classified setting discuss. This is for the safety and security of the ongoing operations of our U.S. military. It is imperative that we do this so that we do not allow insurgents and other enemies of the United States of America to gain an operational advantage. We will adhere to that.

I will assure you that as representatives, we have had classified briefings, and if we have to have additional classified briefings, we will, so members can ask their questions. The Department of Defense and the witnesses here today understand this.

We are—while we have five witnesses here today, I believe we're going to have three opening statements, so we're going to give great liberty to the fact that some of these have been combined. And I believe we're going to start first with Mr. Reid. Please go ahead. Proceed.

WITNESS STATEMENTS

STATEMENT OF GARRY REID

Mr. REID. Thank you, Chairman Chaffetz, Ranking Member Tierney and distinguished members of the subcommittee, thank you for the opportunity to appear before you today. I'm here in the capacity as a senior defense official with oversight of our special operations, but I'm also here, and I bring to that job my background of 28 years of service in the U.S. Army in the Special Operations Forces working very closely with the organizations that we'll be talking about today. I'm joined by a team of civilian and military subject matter experts to honor the fallen of Extortion 17 and to answer your questions.

The downing of Extortion 17 was a catastrophic and unprecedented tragedy for our Nation. As you indicated, Chairman, sadly since 2001, there have been 1,795 U.S. military personnel killed in action in Afghanistan. Any loss of our warriors is a grim reminder of the tragedies of war, the violence of combat action, and the perilous lives our forces live each day in defense of our Nation and our values.

Our sadness for their loss, however, cannot be compared to the pain and anguish of our Gold Star families, some of whom are here today. Their sacrifices cannot be measured and their losses can never be replaced. We are deeply humbled to be in their presence, and hope our testimony can answer their questions, and in some small measure, hope to bring them an additional amount of comfort.

Above all, we are here to pay respect to our fallen heroes and pay tribute to their ultimate sacrifice and honor their service.

Again, chairman, as you indicated, on August 5th, 2011, the brave men of Extortion 17 embarked on an important mission, as they had done so many times before. They were part of a highly capable task force that had conducted more than 2,800 operations in Afghanistan in the previous 12 months using tactics and methods proven in over 10 years of combat against the Taliban and Al Qaeda in Afghanistan.

Tragically, as Extortion 17 was nearing its landing zone, Taliban fighters, hidden in a building, fired two or three rocket-propelled grenades at close range, leaving the pilot no chance to perform evasive maneuvers. One rocket struck a rotor blade, causing the aircraft to crash almost instantly.

The recovery operation commenced immediately and lasted 4 days. All of the fallen were recovered within hours, and ultimately nearly all of the wreckage was recovered. Contrary to some unofficial statements, there was no flight data recorder, no so-called black box. This equipment is not standard on this aircraft.

All of the fallen were taken to Bagram Air Base. A solemn memorial service marked the beginning of a dignified and respectful journey home for the brave men of Extortion 17. A U.S. military chaplain paid tribute to the fallen, as did both the commander of the U.S. task force and the Afghan special operations unit involved in the crash.

An investigation was launched immediately, completed within 30 days, and I'd just like to highlight some of the results and conclusions of that investigation. We believe our forces employed sound tactics in planning and executing their fateful mission. Their high tempo operations paced over the previous months was essential to maintaining pressure on the enemy, and their success in past operations validated the effectiveness of their tactics.

We believe the attachment of the Afghan soldiers enhances the potential for mission success. This specially selected group attached to our task force make invaluable additions to their capabilities, having superior knowledge of the operating environment, the cultural differences, and of course, the native language capability.

We do not believe the special operations variant of the Chinook and air crew would have fared any differently than Extortion 17 on that night. There is no technology advantage inherent in the special operations model that would have protected it from the rocket that downed the aircraft.

We recognize, however, that these helicopters are vulnerable to rocket-propelled grenades. Although there is currently no proven system to counter that particular weapon and that particular enemy tactic, in the 2½ years since this tragic loss, we have fielded 24 different survivability and safety equipment upgrades on over 2,000 of our military aircraft, with the Chinook CH–47 receiving as many as four of these individual upgrades, and we continue our efforts with the support of Congress to fund the research and development to develop the countermeasures that we would need to protect against the RPG. But I have to say no advances in technology, or any change in the way we operate will bring back our fallen heroes or ease the pain of their loved ones. We honor their sacrifices by continuing to dedicate ourselves to defending the nation from attack, upholding our values as Americans and remembering the families left behind. Through our enduring commitment to these Gold Star families, we will cherish the sacrifices of the fallen and keep them forever in our hearts.

Chairman, Ranking Member, I stand ready to address your questions. Thank you very much.

Mr. CHAFFETZ. Thank you.

[Prepared statement of Mr. Reid follows:]

Statement By

Garry Reid, Principal Deputy Assistant Secretary of Defense,

Special Operations and Low Intensity Conflict, United States Department of Defense

Submitted to

The United States House of Representatives

Committee on Oversight and Government Reform

Subcommittee on National Security

Hearing on

Afghanistan: Honoring the Heroes of Extortion 17,

The U.S. CH-47D Aircraft Shot Down in Wardak Province, Afghanistan on August 6, 2011,

Resulting in the deaths of 30 U.S. and Eight Afghan Military Personnel

February 27th, 2014

Chairman Chaffetz, Ranking Member Tierney, and distinguished members of the subcommittee, I appreciate the opportunity to appear before you today to examine the events following the loss of 30 U.S. Service Members, eight Afghans, and a U.S. military working dog aboard a U.S. military CH-47D Chinook helicopter, call sign "Extortion 17" that was shot down by a rocket propelled grenade while conducting combat operations in Wardak Province, Afghanistan on August 6th, 2011.

As a senior U.S. government official, I share in the sacred trust placed upon the Department of Defense by the families and loved ones of our brave servicemen and women to ensure they have the resources, policies, and oversight they need to protect our country from terrorist attacks like those of September 11, 2001 on the World Trade Center and the Pentagon. As a former Special Operations soldier, I understand the risks we ask our service members to take. Since 9/11, there have been 1,795 U.S. military personnel killed and 19,665 wounded in action in Afghanistan.[1] The loss of our comrades in arms is a grim reminder of the tragedies of war, the violence of combat action, and the perilous lives they live each day in defense of our nation and our values.

My sadness, however, cannot be compared to the pain and anguish of our Gold Star families, some of whom are here today. Their sacrifices cannot be measured, their grief cannot be washed away, and their loss can never be replaced. I am deeply humbled to be in their presence, and I hope my testimony today can help answer their questions and in some small measure help bring them comfort. Above all, I am here to respect our fallen heroes, pay tribute to their ultimate sacrifice, and honor their service.

---

[1] Source: Source: U.S. Department of Defense, 26 February 2014, < http://www.defense.gov/news/casualty.pdf>

Eleven U.S. servicemen aboard Extortion 17 entered the military after the 9/11 attacks, answering the call to arms as so many brave Americans have done throughout the history of our great republic. Navy Petty Officer Nicholas Spehar, age 24, of St. Paul, Minnesota, the youngest SEAL in the group, was only 14 when the U.S. was attacked by al-Qa'ida. At just 21 years old, Army Specialist Spencer Duncan of Olathe, Kansas, a crewman on the Chinook helicopter, was the youngest on board. At 47, Army Chief Warrant Officer David Carter, of Centennial, Colorado, was the oldest. Many on board Extortion 17 had completed numerous deployments to Iraq and Afghanistan, taking the fight to a vicious and determined enemy, and denying that enemy the chance to achieve its goal of attacking us again at home. The U.S. did not ask for this war – and although the horrific imagery of 9/11 may have faded from our memories, we cannot forget why we are fighting in Afghanistan. The Taliban hosted al-Qa'ida, allowed Usama Bin Laden to build his organization, and use Afghanistan as a launching pad to destroy the World Trade Center, attack the Pentagon, attempt to destroy the Capitol or the White House and kill 2,996 innocent people, mostly Americans.[2] If given the opportunity, they and those who follow them would try – and have tried - to attack us again.

Qari Tahir, the man our forces were attempting to capture or kill on August 5th, 2011, is one of many Taliban leaders who dedicate their lives to a corrupt agenda that seeks to eliminate freedom, equality, and prosperity in exchange for a medieval society built on violent extremism and wanton destruction. In mid-2011, he took command of the Tangi Valley, sitting at the top of a syndicate of sub-commanders to plan, organize, and conduct attacks on U.S. and Coalition

---

[2] "We Have Some Planes." 9/11 Commission Report. National Commission on Terrorist Attacks Upon the United States. 2004. Retrieved October 1, 2013.

forces. His area of operations in Wardak Province is just 50 miles from Kabul, the capital of Afghanistan. The Taliban place a premium on conducting spectacular attacks in Kabul to terrorize Afghans that support the government, and to kill U.S. and coalition forces. Capturing Qari Tahir would have given us valuable intelligence on plans for these attacks, and enabled more operations to dismantle the Taliban.

The U.S. Navy SEAL task force assigned to conduct operations in Tangi Valley was well conditioned to the dangerous operating environment. In mid-2011, combined with a U.S. Army aviation battalion, they had spent weeks conducting operations nearly every other night in Wardak and surrounding provinces south of Kabul to capture or kill Taliban forces, disrupt attack plots, and deny them sanctuary on this strategic approach to Kabul City.

Intelligence on August 5th indicated Qari Tahir was in Tangi Valley, just a short helicopter flight from the SEAL base camp. The Tangi Valley is strategic terrain that connects the two primary highways that lead to Kabul. The Kabul-Gazni highway defines the north end of the valley, and the Kabul-Gardez highway defines the southern end. The north end of the valley is only a couple of hundred meters wide, closely surrounded by mountain peaks on each side. The Tangi River winds through the valley southeast for about 10 miles, on the southern end the valley widens to more than four miles across. Melting snow from the high mountains to the north and west in central Afghanistan, and the occasion mountain rain shower, create a fertile valley floor that supports farming of apples and pomegranates.

Upon learning of Tahir's possible location, a team of U.S. Army Rangers and Afghan Special Forces was deployed into the valley from the south. At 10:58 p.m., they were inserted by the same CH-47D helicopters that would later conduct the mission to insert the SEAL team. As the operation got underway, our airborne Intelligence, Surveillance and Reconnaissance (ISR) platforms, including an MQ-9 Predator, detected a group evading the Rangers, moving towards the north. AC-130 gunships orbiting overhead directed two AH-64 Apache attack helicopters to fire on and kill five enemy fighters. After some time another group of about 10 Taliban fighters was spotted that we suspected could be Qari Tahir himself fleeing the scene. The SEAL task force was monitoring this activity, and they were soon called upon to deploy quickly into the northern end of the valley to intercept Tahir and capture him and those moving with him. The SEAL commander assembled his force: 17 Navy SEALs, five Navy combat support specialists, three U.S. Air Force Special Tactics Airmen, seven Afghan Special Forces operators, an Afghan interpreter, and a military working dog. The Afghan soldiers were an essential part of the package; they are trained to move with our forces to the target, and when tactical conditions allow initiate operations by calling out enemy forces. This tactic was highly successful; over a period of years hundreds of operations were conducted without firing a shot.

After completing mission planning, and conducting coordination with the aviation unit, the SEAL Task Force moved to the CH-47s to commence the operation. At 2:22 a.m., on August 6th, Extortion 16 and Extortion 17 took off for the short flight to the selected landing zone, circling around the north side of the mountains to enter Tangi valley from the opposite direction used by the Rangers, with intent to surprise the evading enemy element. To expedite unloading at their intended landing zone, all of the SEALs and Afghans boarded Extortion 17, with a crew of five U.S. Army aviators. Extortion 16 accompanied them part of the way to the target, and orbited a few miles away waiting for Extortion 17 to insert the assault force. As they advanced, the AC-130 and a suite of airborne intelligence platforms scanned the valley to overwatch the Rangers, who were still conducting their operation. The Apaches, flying in "detached escort" mode, approached from the south to check the landing zone for enemy presence, and scan the ingress route to detect any threats. They saw none.

At 2:38 a.m., Extortion 17 indicated they were one minute from the landing zone. As they slowed to land, Taliban fighters hidden on top of a building on the west side of the valley fired two or three rocket propelled grenades at the helicopter. The attackers, who had not been detected by the two Apaches, the Predator or the AC-130, were well positioned at the most narrow area of the valley, only 200 meters wide and serving to funnel a low flying, incoming helicopter right past the building they occupied. Although there was no moonlight and little illumination from the nearby village, they were able to hear and see the Chinook as it entered the valley, shooting at it from nearly head-on at a distance of less than 250 yards, leaving the pilot no chance to perform evasive maneuvers. Traveling at 120 yards per second as it leaves the launcher, the velocity of the RPG round, combined with the airspeed of the oncoming Chinook, left the pilot with less than one second to identify the threat, react and maneuver the 40,000 pound loaded helicopter. Evasive action was not possible. One rocket struck a rotor blade, causing the aircraft to spin violently, and crash almost instantly into a dry creek bed. The main fuselage was immediately engulfed in flames. Extortion 17 was down, and there were no signs of survivors. Apaches scanned the area for enemy, and fired its cannon along a tree line to prevent anyone access to the burning CH-47. The Ranger element was quickly alerted to converge on the crash site. A 20 man Pathfinder unit was alerted and deployed to secure the site. As daybreak reached the valley, the solemn task of recovering our fallen heroes began. All 30 Americans and 8 Afghans on Extortion 17 had perished.

The recovery operation in a hostile operating environment lasted four days. All of the fallen were recovered within hours, but the wreckage was spread over a large area when the shattered rotor blades broke from their pylons upon impact by the RPG. The main fuselage was situated in a creek bed, and parts of the wreckage were swept a hundred meters down stream by a flash flood on the evening of August 6th. Ultimately nearly all of the wreckage was recovered. There was no flight recorder - this equipment is not standard on the CH-47D.

The fallen U.S. service members were taken to Bagram Air Base. Joined by their Afghan comrades, these brave warriors were paid honors by their fellow unit members, commanders, and coalition partners. A solemn memorial service marked the beginning of a dignified and respectful journey home for the brave men of Extortion 17. Consistent with our warrior ethos that no man will be left behind, all of the fallen; Navy SEALs and Combat Support specialists, Army aviators, Air Force Air Commandos, and Afghan soldiers all were equally memorialized in a combined service. All paid the ultimate price for freedom, and all deserved to be honored and respected. The commander of the U.S. Special Operations task force and a U.S. military chaplain paid tribute to the fallen, as did the Commander of the Afghan Special Forces.

As soon as this tragic incident occurred, our military leaders, planners, and operators began asking the question - "How did this happen?" General James Mattis, Commander of the

U.S. Central Command, immediately tasked an experienced General Officer to conduct a full investigation to determine the facts and circumstances surrounding the crash, the cause of the crash, any recommendations concerning improvements to tactics, techniques, and procedures to improve our operations, and any other matters pertaining to the incident the investigating officer deemed relevant. The investigating officer rendered his report a month later, complete with 86 exhibits full of supporting technical data, transcribed interviews with those involved in the planning of the mission and execution of the recovery operation, historical records of aircraft maintenance, crew qualifications, and other pertinent information.

What have we learned from this tragedy, and how does the Department of Defense assessment differ from some views expressed in the public domain?

We believe the SEAL task force employed sound tactics in planning and executing their fateful mission, including the decision to load the entire element on a single aircraft. Their high-tempo operations pace over the previous months was essential to maintaining pressure on the Taliban, and their success in past operations validated the effectiveness of their tactics, techniques, and procedures. Employing the SEALs, Rangers, Army aviation, and Afghan soldiers into a combined team reflects the best practices of our "combined joint task force" approach that has served as the model of success for more than 12 years of war since 2001.

We believe the attachment of Afghan soldiers to the SEAL task force, and the process for coordinating our operations with the Afghan military leadership, enhances the potential for mission success. The Afghan teams are invaluable additions to our force – having superior knowledge of the operating environment, cultural nuances, and native language capability. The force attached to the SEALs is specially trained for these operations, and they have been partnered with U.S. Special Operations assault elements for the past several years. When the U.S. military mission in Afghanistan is over the Afghan forces will continue to provide security and conduct operations to counter the Taliban insurgency. The U.S. cannot stay in Afghanistan indefinitely providing security; we will cease combat operations at the end of 2014. To ensure long term stability in Afghanistan we must train and mentor Afghan forces now, so they can develop the capability to operate without us later.

We believe the Army CH-47D aircraft and crews were suitable and proper for this mission. Our Chinook pilots and crew carefully planned their route consistent with proven tactics, deliberately altering their route to enter the valley from a different direction than had been used earlier that night. They masked their approach by circling around the valley to the northeast, and dropped down to a low altitude on final ingress to the selected landing zone.

We do not believe a Special Operations Chinook and aircrew (MH-47) would have fared differently than the CH-47D flown by the Extortion 17 crew. As noted by the investigating officer, the Extortion 17 crew was experienced flying in the Tangi Valley – and inserted the Ranger unit earlier in the evening. The short flight route was over familiar terrain, with no air defense radar threat, obviating the need for the high-tech avionics package that distinguishes the MH-47 from the CH-47. The two models share identical Threat Countermeasures and Aircraft Survivability Equipment – meaning there is no technology advantage inherent in the MH-47 that would have protected it from the rocket that downed Extortion 17.

We do not believe Extortion 17 was the victim of a pre-planned enemy ambush, nor do we believe the enemy had advance knowledge of our flight route and landing zone location. This information was not provided to anyone outside the SEAL and Army aviation task force commands. Because the mission was developed and approved after the Ranger assault had begun, there was no coordination with Afghan officials. Although the presence of helicopters in the valley likely put the enemy forces on a heightened state of alert, the element that fired the rockets remained undetected by our airborne sensors until unleashing its fatal volley as Extortion 17 was nearing the designated landing zone.

We do not believe the rules of engagement restricted our forces from engaging the enemy during this operation. The AH-64 Apache helicopters that comprised the Air Weapons Team performed their escort duties consistent with proven tactics, demonstrating sound judgment at each stage of the operation from the time the Ranger element entered the Tangi Valley until all U.S. forces were extracted following recovery operations at the crash site.

We recognize our helicopters are vulnerable to direct fire from Rocket Propelled Grenade (RPG) and other shoulder fired ballistic rockets. Tragically Extortion 17 is not the first Chinook helicopter lost to RPG fire in Afghanistan. Sixteen Special Operators, including eight SEALs, perished in a similar incident involving an MH-47 in Kunar Province in June 2005, and in March 2002 an MH-47 was shot with an RPG, resulting in the first SEAL fatality of the war in Afghanistan.

Immediately after the loss of Extortion 17, the Assistant Secretary of Defense for Research and Engineering directed the Helicopter Survivability Task Force (HSTF), established in August 2009, to examine in detail potential countermeasures to rocket-propelled grenade (RPG) attacks. A surge effort involving more than 80 government personnel, including 23 nationally-recognized subject matter experts assessed technological solutions to this threat, including concepts of varying maturity from 17 industry teams. Unfortunately, the findings of this assessment were that technologies to enable the development of Active Protection Systems (APS) for helicopters are immature and unproven.

Subsequent to this effort, the Director for Operational Test and Evaluation delivered a report to Congress in February 2012 regarding the maturity of Active Protection Systems (APS) for Ground Vehicles. The findings of that report were that none of the seven tested systems were mature enough for fielding; further development, test, and evaluation was required for ALL of the systems. Given the severity of the RPG threat to rotorcraft, DOD has continued to actively research RPG Active Protection Systems for aircraft.

We recognize more needs to be done to help protect our forces – especially when they are so vulnerable in the air. In the two and half years since this tragic loss, HSTF efforts, supported by three reprogramming actions worth over $182 million approved by Congress, have resulted in the fielding of 24 different survivability and safety equipment upgrades on over 2,000 aircraft, with CH-47s receiving as many as four of these individual upgrades.[3,4] Every rotorcraft operating in Afghanistan has received at least two of these upgrades, and some have received as

---

[3] Over 3000 individual aircraft equipment upgrades were performed as a result of the HSTF efforts.
[4] Source: PA 10-3, March 2010; PA 10-24, Oct 2010; PA 11-25, Oct 2011

many as five. The Department continues to actively pursue the accelerated fielding of RPG
Active Protection Systems on rotary wing aircraft.

Although we will continue to develop the best equipment to protect our brave service men
and women, sadly there is no technological solution that will guarantee the safety of those thrust
into battle, particularly when helicopters are involved.   Afghanistan is especially dangerous
given the high elevations and mountainous terrain. Our aviators have responded and performed
brilliantly during this war, but the fact remains we will always have to balance the tactical
requirement to move troops quickly across the battlefield with the dangers of incurring lethal
enemy fire and flying in extreme terrain.

No advances in technology, or changes in the way we operate, will bring back our fallen
heroes or ease the pain of their loved ones. We honor their sacrifices by rededicating ourselves
to defending the nation from attack, upholding our values as Americans, and never forgetting
those they left behind.   Through our enduring commitment to our Gold Star families; the
mothers and fathers, sisters and brothers, extended families, wives and children of the 30 Fallen
Eagles aboard Extortion 17, we will cherish their memories, keep them forever in our hearts, and
never forget them.

I stand ready to address your questions.

Mr. CHAFFETZ. Ms. Skillman.

STATEMENT OF DEBORAH SKILLMAN

Ms. SKILLMAN. Chairman Chaffetz, Ranking Member Tierney, and distinguished members of the committee, I want to thank you for the opportunity to appear before you today to answer your questions regarding our assistance to surviving family members of these 30 brave heroes who were killed in action on August 6th, 2011.

I am the program manager for Casualty and Mortuary Affairs within the Office of the Secretary of Defense. In this capacity, I am responsible for providing uniform policies and procedures to the military departments for notifying and assisting the next of kin of service members who have become a casualty. My office is also the focal point for the coordination of all matters related to our Mortuary Affairs programs.

As a little background on myself, I am a retired army colonel with over 12 years experience working in this particular program.

The Department holds casualty and Mortuary Affairs program among our most solemn responsibilities to our service members, our surviving family members, and to our Nation. A fundamental element of military culture and tradition is that we hold our fallen in the highest esteem, treat their remains with highest reverence and provide their surviving family members the highest level of care and continued support. My office is responsible for promulgating casualty and Mortuary Affairs policies that reflect these core values, and we work in coordination with the service members and the colleagues, my colleagues that you see at the table here today, to ensure that the intent of our policies is reflected throughout all casualty and mortuary tasks and processes.

If I could just take a moment about some of the testimony you will hear today and some common terminology that my colleagues will be using. We will be discussing the DD Form 93. This is the record of emergency data. And I want to note that the DD Form 93 is the voice of the service member upon his or her death. This form is completed by all service members at regular intervals during their military service, and informs the casualty offices of whom the service member wishes to be notified in the event he or she becomes a casualty.

The form also indicates whom the service member wishes to receive certain death benefits, and it allows the service member to designate the Person Authorized to Direct Disposition, or the PADD. It's worth noting that the service member can select anyone as the PADD, not necessarily a family member. And the PADD is the single person that the casualty office may take direction from regarding the disposition of the service member's remains.

Before I pass it over to my colleague, Colonel Devillier, sir, my colleagues in the Army and the Navy Casualty Office have also prepared a statement, and I request that they be allowed to provide that for the record.

Ms. SKILLMAN. Again, I want to thank you for the opportunity to appear before you today, and it's my honor and my privilege to serve in this capacity, and I hope today we'll be able to address your concerns.

Mr. CHAFFETZ. Thank you. And thank you for your service and your caring. And, of course, we will enter that into the record. Colonel?

STATEMENT OF COLONEL JOHN DEVILLIER

Colonel DEVILLIER. Chairman Chaffetz, Ranking Member Tierney and distinguished members of the subcommittee, I appreciate the opportunity to appear before you today to discuss the process of disposition of our fallen heroes from Extortion 17.

Since March 2012, I have had the honor and privilege to serve with some of the finest soldiers, sailors, airmen, marines and civilians who work behind the scenes providing dignity, honor and respect to our Nation's combat fallen as well as care, service and support to their families.

While the port mortuary has been associated with Dover Air Force Base, Delaware, since the 1950s, the organization I command was activated in early 2009 in response to Department of Defense directed changes surrounding authorized family travel to Dover Air Force Base and media access to dignified transfer. My organization has both Air Force specific rules, along with being the lead service component for dignified transfers and effecting final disposition of our fallen as directed by the Person Authorized to Direct Disposition, the PADD.

Since the implementation of policy changes in April 2009, team Dover has welcomed home over 1,800 of our Nation's fallen and supported over 8,700 of their families.

The events surrounding the return of the fallen from Extortion 17 are seen as a watershed for our operation at Dover in terms of mass fatalities. Team Dover has supported well over 800 family, friends and unit members, as well as more than 40 distinguished visitors desiring to pay their respects to these brave heroes.

While I was not present for this event, it was a monumental undertaking for the entire team in terms of support. As with every fallen service member who arrives at Dover, the fallen from this event were taken into the medical-legal custody of the Armed Forces medical examiner system for scientific identification, which may include fingerprinting, dental and/or DNA testing followed by a medical autopsy. Upon the scientific identification, the chain of custody for the fallen is then passed to my organization to effect final disposition, as directed by the PADD.

For this incident as a whole, my organization effected these disposition instructions for our 30 heroes, eight of which included written requests for cremation from the PADD. For those eight cases, four were cremated at the port mortuary, and four were cremated at their final resting place.

Again, we consider this incident a watershed moment and we have made a number of changes in terms of our in place support mechanisms. In January 2013, we opened a new command and control facility to enhance communication between the branches of service and my organization. Additionally in February 2013, a new chapel was opened on Dover with one-third of the space dedicated to our operation in terms of facilities to further support families.

In my nearly 21 years of active military service, I have never served in a more honorable or humbling mission. The men and women who work tirelessly behind the scenes under my command see the worst results of conflict. Not only do they honor the fallen, they serve the families, who are often experiencing the worst moments of their life, and these quiet professionals ask for nothing in return. I'm proud to serve as their commander.

Thank you for your time this morning and your strong support for the men and women of the Department of the Air Force.

Mr. CHAFFETZ. Thank you, Colonel.

[The statement of Colonel Devillier follows:]

United States Air Force

Presentation

Before the House Oversight and
Government Reform Committee

Disposition of Remains – Extortion 17

Witness Statement of Colonel John M.
Devillier, Commander, Air Force
Mortuary Affairs Operations

February 27,
2014

Chairman Chaffetz, Representative Tierney, and distinguished members of the subcommittee, I appreciate the opportunity to appear before you today to discuss the process of disposition of remains from Extortion 17. Since March 2012 I have had the honor and privilege to serve with some of the finest Soldiers, Sailors, Airmen, Marines, and Civilians who work behind the scenes as quiet professionals to provide dignity, honor, and respect to our nation's combat fallen as well as care, service, and support to their families.

While the Port Mortuary has been associated with Dover Air Force Base, Delaware since the 1950s, the organization I command, Air Force Mortuary Affairs Operations, was activated in early 2009 in response to Department of Defense directed changes surrounding authorized family travel to Dover Air Force Base and media access to Dignified Transfers. My organization has both Air Force specific roles along with being the lead service component for Dignified Transfers, Media Policy, and effecting final disposition of our fallen as directed by the Person Authorized to Direct Disposition. While we are an Air Force organization, our sister services provide liaison teams who work in our facility to support their individual service fallen and the families of these fallen. Currently our team consists of just over 100 Soldiers, Sailors, Airmen, Marines, and Civilians serving within the Charles C. Carson Center for Mortuary Affairs at Dover Air Force Base.

For our Air Force specific role, we provide subject matter expertise to the entire Air Force in the areas of mortuary entitlements as outlined in statute, general honor guard policy, and we also serve as a direct link to families of airmen still unaccounted for from Korea, Vietnam, and the Cold War. Furthermore, we serve as mortuary officers for airmen who are killed in overseas operations, providing direct assistance to their families in terms of travel to Dover for Dignified Transfers and assisting these families with mortuary entitlements and associated disposition instructions. In our lead service component role, my team executes all Dignified Transfers as well as implements media policy for those Dignified Transfers. Additionally, we serve as the only continental United States Port Mortuary and in conjunction with our sister services we prepare and ship all of our nation's fallen to their final destination, regardless of branch of service. Lastly, given the size of the mortuary and our co-location with the Armed Forces Medical Examiner System, we are tasked with supporting mass fatalities as directed by the leadership of the Department of Defense.

Since the implementation of policy changes in April 2009, Team Dover has welcomed home 1,820 of our nation's fallen (military, civilian, and contractors) and supported 8,706 of their families at Dover. Families travel to Dover to welcome home their loved one for 83 percent of our Dignified Transfers, and families elect some level of media coverage in 90 percent of these Dignified Transfers. Since April 2009, we have supported 52 mass fatality events, defined as a single event with 5 or more casualties.

The events surrounding the return of the fallen from the CH-47 incident in August 2011 are seen as a watershed for our operation at Dover in terms of mass fatalities. In this incident, we received 38 fallen of which 22 were Sailors, 5 were Soldiers, 3 were Airmen, and 8 were Afghan nationals. Team Dover supported well over 800 family, friends, and unit members as well as more than 40 distinguished visitors, to include the President of the United States, the Secretary of Defense, Service Secretaries, and others desiring to pay their respects to these brave individuals. While I was not present for this event in 2011, it was a monumental undertaking for the entire team in terms of support.

As with every fallen service member who arrives at Dover, the fallen from this event were taken into the medical-legal custody of the Armed Forces Medical Examiner System for scientific identification, which may include finger printing, dental, and/or DNA testing followed by a medical autopsy. Upon the scientific identification, the chain of custody for the fallen is then passed to my organization to effect final disposition. For each case, the branch of service of the fallen, interacting with the Person Authorized to Direct Disposition, provides written instructions for final disposition, which my organization then executes.

For the three airmen involved in the incident, the Person Authorized to Direct Disposition (PADD) were initially briefed at the Center for the Families of the Fallen at Dover AFB prior to the dignified transfer. The briefing included the dignified transfer process, an entitlements briefing, and a review/completion of the AF Form 970, Statement of Disposition of Remains. Through this form, the PADD provided written instructions for disposition of their loved one to the Air Force, regardless of the condition of the remains. Upon receipt of the remains from the Armed Forces Medical Examiner, the licensed funeral directors who performed the embalming process made a recommendation of viewability via DD Form 2063. In all three cases, the funeral director responsible for the embalming recommended the remains be considered non-viewable. Given the fragmented condition of the remains, an additional form was required from the PADD of these three airmen, the Central Joint Mortuary Affairs Board Form One in which the PADD provided specific instructions regarding any additional remains found of their loved one. This form is required when the Armed Forces Medical Examiner determines the remains are considered non-intact. These written instructions were then executed by the Port Mortuary to return the fallen as expeditiously as possible to their final destination.

For the Extortion 17 incident as a whole, my organization effected these disposition instructions for our 30 heroes, 8 of which included requests for cremation from the PADD. For those 8 cases, 4 were cremated at the Port Mortuary, and 4 were cremated at their final resting place. Regardless of the size of the incident in question, the internal process for receiving and then executing disposition instructions has remained unaltered since this event with the exception of a change implemented in 2012 where we no longer perform full body cremations at Dover. Cremations now occur only at the final destination through a funeral home directed by the PADD.

Again, we consider this incident a watershed moment because of the size and scope of the event, particularly in terms of family support. Prior to 2009, families could travel to Dover but it was at their own expense, thus, in past cases, while families traveled to Dover, the numbers were relatively small. Based upon this incident, we have made a number of changes in terms of our in place support mechanisms. In January 2013 we opened a new command and control facility to enhance communication between the branches of service and my organization for mass fatality situations. This command and control cell is staffed 24 hours a day, 7 days a week, 365 days a year. Additionally, in February 2013, a new chapel was opened on Dover, with one-third of the space dedicated to our operation in terms of facilities to further support families during a mass fatality event.

In my nearly 21 years of active military service, I have never served in a more honorable or humbling mission. The men and women who work tirelessly behind the scenes at the Charles C. Carson Center for Mortuary Affairs at Dover Air Force Base see the worst side of conflict. Not only do they honor the fallen, they serve the families who are often experiencing the worst moments of their life. These silent professionals ask for nothing in return and I'm proud to serve as their commander. Thank you for your strong support of the men and women of the Department of the Air Force.

Mr. CHAFFETZ. Colonel Brown.

STATEMENT OF COLONEL KERK BROWN

Colonel BROWN. Chairman Chaffetz, Ranking Member Tierney and other distinguished members of the subcommittee, thank you for the opportunity to represent the United States Army, and I am humbled to provide testimony in honor of the service members of Extortion 17.

I have served as the director of the Army Casualty & Mortuary Affairs Operations Center since July 2012. The mission of the Casualty & Mortuary Affairs Operations Center is to execute the full spectrum of Army Casualty & Mortuary Affairs for present and past conflicts. In this role, the Casualty & Mortuary Affairs Operations Center provides policy and direction to 33 casualty assistance centers around the world, develops standardized casualty assistance and casualty notification training, provides notification, casualty assistance and casualty management for injured, ill, missing and deceased personnel, and operates the joint personal effects depot at Dover Air Force Base for all of the services.

On August 6th, 2011, five soldiers were killed in action in support of the Extortion 17 mission. The notification and assistance provided to the soldiers' next of kin were completed in accordance with policy. The Army recognizes that people are the Army, and our dedicated and talented force is the reason the United States Army is second to none. The Army remains committed to honor our Nation's commitment to its soldiers and the family of deceased, injured, ill and unaccounted for through compassionate and responsive support.

Thank you for your continued support to the United States Army, and I look forward to answering your questions.

Mr. CHAFFETZ. Thank you, Colonel.

STATEMENT OF COMMANDER AARON BRODSKY

Commander BRODSKY. Chairman Chaffetz, Ranking Member Tierney, other distinguished members, good morning. I'm Director of Navy Casualty & Mortuary Affairs at the Navy Personnel Command in Millington, Tennessee. Thank you also for this opportunity.

I've been director of Navy Casualty since August 2013. My office is lead for the Navy Casualty's assistance program, which includes next of kin verification, execution of proper and timely notifications, and benefits and entitlements authorizations. We do this across three command tiers: Navy Personnel Command, consisting of program management, entitlements execution and casualty aftercare; Commander Naval Installations Command, which is 24/7 operations through regional operations centers; and the Casualty Assistance Calls Officer, or CACO, training and assignment, and, of course, our network of more than 6,000 trained CACOs worldwide.

I'm here today to discuss navy protocol and procedures with regards to casualty assistance, and I will also discuss the manner in which casualty assistance was rendered to the families of the 22 Navy personnel who perished on Extortion 17.

When the Navy first learned of the Extortion 17 incident on August 6th, 2011, all established protocols and procedures were initiated, next of kin were verified, and regional CACOs were assigned. Within a few hours, the extent of this casualty became fully known. At this point, Naval Special Warfare Development Group and Special Operations Command teamed with Navy Casualty, and together trained CACOs and command representatives notified each next of kin and provided follow-on assistance to all the families and their authorized beneficiaries.

The special warfare community is unfortunately well versed in casualty assistance, and within the first 24 hours, they established a casualty assistance and call center and created casualty teams for each family. This command and control structure complemented our own and provided not only an increase in capability and capacity, but also lent their expertise and professional insight.

To echo my colleagues, at the end of the day, we all want the same thing: timely and compassionate care for our grieving Gold Star families. The assistance rendered to Navy families is professionally and compassionately conducted, always prioritizing their needs for the acute sensitivity for the profound grief they experience.

On behalf of Navy leadership and the men and women in the United States Navy and their families, I thank you as well for your commitment to these heroes of Extortion 17, and I look forward to your questions.

Mr. CHAFFETZ. Thank you, Commander. Appreciate it.

I now recognize—I have actually some unanimous consent requests. The first request I have is to place into the record the statements of Mary Strange, Terry Pittman, Ida Pittman, Charlie Strange and Doug Hamburger.

Mr. TIERNEY. No objection.

Mr. CHAFFETZ. Without objection, so ordered. I also ask unanimous consent to enter into the record DD Form 33, that was mentioned in part of the testimony. Or 93, sorry. Without—without objection?

Mr. TIERNEY. No objection.

Mr. CHAFFETZ. So ordered. I'll now recognize myself for 5 minutes.

Mr. Reid, without touching into the—into the classified information, what can you tell us about why this mission was happening and what they were trying to do, why they were engaged in this? And, again, I recognize the limitations you have no classified setting, but if you could set the context, I would appreciate it.

Mr. REID. Thank you, chairman. The objective on this night was to capture a senior Taliban commander operating in a valley that cuts between two main highways south of Kabul, the capital of Afghanistan. The strategic relevance of this valley is it provides the Taliban with a sanctuary and a jumping-off point. Their goal is to conduct spectacular attacks in Kabul, to terrorize Afghans that support the government and support the coalition, and to attack our—our bases there. That's the strategic context of this particular mission, as a part of a broader campaign, as you know, chairman, to dismantle and defeat these Taliban organizations throughout Afghanistan, to allow the government forces to establish a security foothold and transition out of U.S. combat actions, as we will at the end of this year, into Afghans providing security.

Mr. CHAFFETZ. Now, one of the more troubling and sensational stories that we have seen along the way is the idea that upon this— the crash of the helicopter after it was shot is that the black box was supposedly washed away in a flash flood, which defies— I mean, it's really hard to believe. We have talked about this, but could you please respond to that story, because it has been out there fairly—fairly pervasively.

Mr. REID. Yes, Chairman. Thank you. This valley, as I said, in— situated in between these mountains is part of a drainage system that feeds over into the central highlands of Afghanistan over the Uruzgan Province. The elevation in this particular valley is around 7,000 feet, but it is a drainage area for high mountain showers and snow melt. It's actually a very fertile valley with a large amount of agriculture.

On the night of August 6th, as we were one day into the recovery effort, a flash flood swept through the valley. The aircraft, upon crashing, landed in a dry creek bed. That creek bed filled with up to 4 feet of water very quickly during the recovery effort, and some of the material from the crash was washed about 100 yards downstream.

We—we have a photograph board. If we could light like up——

Mr. CHAFFETZ. If you can like that up. Sure.

Mr. REID. —to enter that, sir, we can show the before and after.

Mr. CHAFFETZ. I think we're just going to show the flash flood.

Mr. REID. Yes.

Mr. CHAFFETZ. We're not going to show the actual wreckage itself.

The idea that the black box washed away, was there a black box?

Mr. REID. No, sir, not—as I indicated, there is a device attached to the engines that records engine performance. It's—the engines are new, in fact, the same engines that are on the other Chinooks, the modern engines, but the airframe itself is an analog aircraft. There is no source of digital data.

Mr. CHAFFETZ. There is no traditional so-called black box?

Mr. REID. That's correct, sir.

Mr. CHAFFETZ. Even though there was a flash flood, and there are other photos as well that——

Mr. REID. Yes, sir.

Mr. CHAFFETZ. Publicly, this is not something we're revealing and showing for the very first time. This is something that has been—is out there and widely available.

Can I—Ms. Skillman, I want to talk about the ramp ceremony, because the other point—one of the other major points of contention as I've talked to a lot of families is that there is a video of the service that was done in Afghanistan. My understanding is—I have two questions about this, two concerns. One is why it was videotaped. My understanding is that is not what current DOD policy is. My question is, why did that happen? Did it happen? Why did it happen? And who was the person who was making the—who participated in that—in that service, because there were some very concerning comments that were made by the person who was representing the Afghans who were killed that night.

Ms. SKILLMAN. Sir, thank you for the question. I—I cannot address who was speaking at—at the memorial service at that particular ceremony in Bagram.

As we understand, the commanders conducted a memorial service, which is within policy. We expect our commanders to do that. And their interpretation of our policy was that the videotape was—was allowed. However, we have just learned that they recently republished their policy to reflect our considerations for the next of kin and wanting them to consent to any videotaping of their next of kin. So their regulation was revised in February of 2013, which we have just recently learned, to reflect that current policy.

Mr. CHAFFETZ. I have more questions. My time is expired. I'll now recognize the gentleman from Massachusetts, Mr. Tierney.

Mr. TIERNEY. Thank you for that.

Mr. Reid, in your written remarks, you provide a significant amount of detail about the operation of Extortion 17 and, for instance, you mention the Navy SEAL task force and the U.S. Army aviation group, and I quote, ''spent weeks conducting operations nearly every other night.''

You stated the Afghan soldiers deployed with the American Special Forces, and I quote again, ''were an essential part of the package. They are trained to move with our forces to the target, and when tactical conditions allow, initiate operations by calling out enemy forces. This tactic was highly successful over a period of years. Hundreds of operations were conducted without firing a shot.''

You then say the rocket-propelled grenade that brought down Extortion 17, ''left the pilot with less than one second to identify the threat, react and maneuver the 40,000-pound loaded helicopter. Evasive action was not possible.''

And regarding the flight route and the landing zone for Extortion 17, you wrote, ''This information was not provided to anyone outside the SEAL and Army aviation task force commands. Because the mission was developed and approved after the ranger assault had begun, there was no coordination with Afghan officials.''

And finally you state you believe, ''the SEAL task force employed sound tactics in planning and executing their fateful mission, and that you do not believe the rules of engagement restricted our forces from engaging the enemy.''

So, Mr. Reid, with all—we all believe that the downing of Extortion 17 was a tragic loss of life, there's no doubt about that, but how would you characterize the operation that day? Was it hastily or poorly planned as a mission? Were the appropriate teams and equipment used? Was the mission compromised?

Mr. REID. Thank you, Congressman. The mission was planned. This particular—the SEAL mission was planned in the course of the ranger mission, and that planning process is deliberate. And what I mean is their role in this operation was a standby force should there be a necessity to deploy a second force.

The way this worked at that time, they have two forces. They have the SEALs and the rangers. And typically, every other night, every third night, we do an operation, one would be the lead, one would be the standby, and that was the conditions this night. So there was always the condition and the intent to deploy this force based on the tactical circumstance.

And as I indicated, sir, the circumstances were such that the enemy appeared to evade the initial attack and seek sanctuary in the valley in another location. The SEAL mission was constituted to come in from the other direction and intercept that Taliban leader.

We do not believe the mission was compromised. There is a coordination process with Afghan leaders for these missions that was put in place years prior to mitigate against claims of civilian casualties in special operations that were not coordinated. But on this particular event, understanding the SEAL piece was—was done during the operation, there was no external coordination, so there was no possibility of information going up the chain and somehow coming back out to the Taliban.

We believe the enemy positioned himself in that building. Whether or not he knew anyone was coming in, he was in a very advantageous place tactically to strike the aircraft as it approached.

Mr. TIERNEY. Thank you. Thanks, Mr. Reid.

So we just talked a little bit about the concern we had for the treatment of the—of our fallen heroes. Before the bodies were even to reach Dover, they had a transfer ceremony at the Bagram Airfield. That ramp ceremony was conducted to honor those dead servicemen.

Ms. Skillman, it's my understanding that the ramp ceremonies are customary, and that they're solemn and respectful events. Can you explain why the ramp ceremony—or what it is and why it occurred?

Ms. SKILLMAN. Thank you, sir. I—I can't address what happened in theater, however, that we do—commanders routinely conduct what we would consider a memorial service for their fallen, which is exactly what happened on that day.

Mr. TIERNEY. And that's, as I say, customary?

Ms. SKILLMAN. Yes, sir, it is.

Mr. TIERNEY. And it's not customary generally to videotape, as you mentioned to Mr. Chaffetz's question?

Ms. SKILLMAN. No, sir, it is not. It was our intent that next of kin consent to any still photography or videography of their loved ones. Primarily the PNOK is responsible for making that consent, the Primary Next of Kin; however, there's a misinterpretation of our policy, and we have clarified that, and CENTCOM has recently revised their policies, as I stated earlier.

Mr. TIERNEY. Good. Thank you. Yield back, Mr. Chair.

Mr. CHAFFETZ. Thank you. I now recognize the gentlewoman from Wyoming, the vice-chair of our subcommittee, Ms. Lummis, for 5 minutes.

Mrs. LUMMIS. Thank you, Mr. Chairman. I want to extend my appreciation to the next of kin here present of our deceased members of the military who participated in the mission that brought down Extortion 17. We are grateful for your family's service, for your sacrifice, and they will not be forgotten.

I—I also want to comment, Mr. Chairman, on an old 2009 HBO movie called ''Taking Chance'' that was a documentary about a fallen Iraq Veteran, a Marine by the name of Chance Phelps, and it illustrated the treatment that the military provides to our servicemen and women once they have been killed in action, and they are—their remains are being returned to their homes. Chance Phelps, who was the soldier who was killed and whose return to my home State of Wyoming is illustrated in that film, is someone whose parents I knew. My husband and Chance Phelps' father were high school friends and I know his mother very well, and how proud we are that the manner in which he was treated was so well illustrated by the film and how it accurately, we believe, depicted the manner in which and the respect with which his remains were treated by the military. So I want to commend the work of our military services with regard to their very dignified and appropriately respectful treatment of those who gave their last measure of human devotion.

I also would like to follow that up with a question. This is for all witnesses. Did the Department follow protocol and directions from the servicemen's Person Authorized to Direct Disposition of human remains in the case of Extortion 17? Colonel Devillier.

Colonel DEVILLIER. Yes, ma'am. Thank you for that question. In all 30 cases, the direction provided by the—the written direction provided by the PADD was followed appropriately.

Mrs. LUMMIS. And are these records available to reflect that for anyone who might wish to use the Freedom of Information Act to obtain that information?

Colonel DEVILLIER. Ma'am, family members can certainly request that through FOIA, and they would be redacted according to the FOIA rules.

Mrs. LUMMIS. Okay. Would anyone else care to offer perspective on that question? Thank you.

What are some of the guidelines for reporting, recording, notifying and assisting the next of kin whenever DOD casualties are sustained? Once again, I would direct that question to whoever wishes to answer. Ms. Skillman?

Ms. SKILLMAN. Ma'am, thank you for that question. The services are directed to provide standardized training for their notification officers, their casualty assistance officers, and to provide proactive support to family members. They get—they will have a dialogue with the family members that they are assisting and they will proactively provide them with information regarding the circumstances surrounding the death as soon as it becomes available and provide them regular updates. They will also assist them with the benefits request and reports of investigations and then continued follow on care.

Mrs. LUMMIS. Did the Department follow its policies in the case of the families of Extortion 17?

Ms. SKILLMAN. Ma'am, from our records, there's all indication that each of the services followed the policies and procedures as prescribed by DOD.

Mrs. LUMMIS. Okay. Also for you, Ms. Skillman, how can we improve the policies to ensure that families receive all the casualty information to which they are legally entitled?

Ms. SKILLMAN. Ma'am, thank you for that—that question. We are constantly improving our program, and it's through forums such as this, input from our family members, our veterans service organizations, our partner agencies, such as the Department of Veterans Affairs that we make continued improvements.

Mrs. LUMMIS. Thank you. My time has expired.

Mr. CHAFFETZ. Thank the gentlewoman. Now recognize the gentlewoman from New York, Ms. Maloney, for 5 minutes.

Mrs. MALONEY. Thank you, Mr. Chairman and Mr. Ranking Member, and thank you to all the panelists. And before I ask my question, I want to join with all of my colleagues and all the members on this panel to acknowledge the sacrifice made by the fallen heroes as well as the families, some of whom are here today.

And I would like to go back, if I could, to the questioning on the flight recorder, or the so-called black box, and I'd like to ask Mr. Reid, and thank you for your public service. My brother also served in the Special Forces with the Army, and we're very proud of the work of that division for our country. Did you—I believe you answered the question from the chairman that there was no black box. That's correct, that there was no black box?

Mr. REID. Yes, ma'am, that's correct.

Mrs. MALONEY. Well, I want to ask to clarify that. Do other CH–47D's have a black box?

Mr. REID. No, ma'am. The aircraft is not a digital—does not have a suite of digital electronics. It has gauges, analog gauges. Those gauges do not provide you with the ability to withdraw, extract digital data that you could record.

Mrs. MALONEY. Now, today there was a photograph of a flash flood that we saw earlier, but I've received some correspondence to my office that suggested that there was not a flash flood, so I'd like to clarify that a little more. I understand that—that the—that the plane, Extortion 17, crashed into a creek bed. Is that correct?

Mr. REID. Yes, ma'am, that's correct.

Mrs. MALONEY. A dry creek bed. So can you explain for us whether a flash flood occurred in that creek bed? Some people allege that it did not occur, so could you clarify if that——

Mr. REID. Ma'am, I can clarify, having read the report and spoken to individuals involved and seeing the photographs and studied the climate data, from my own assessment, I believe it's perfectly logical and credible that a flood occurred. We had up to 140 people at that site over the period of 4 days, about 45 or 50 within an hour. We never left that site until everything was recovered. Multiple accounts and, again, photographs show the water in the creek that was not there on the first day. It happened on the night of the 6th of August, ma'am.

Mrs. MALONEY. So did the flash flood complicate the recovery?

Mr. REID. It halted the efforts temporarily, because we had to move people to higher ground. But as these occur, even in our own desert southwest area, they—they come very quickly without warning and they recede often just as quickly. As you saw in the photo, though, there was still some residual water, but the majority of the wreckage had been recovered at that time.

Mrs. MALONEY. So it did complicate it. Do you think that going forward, we should have black boxes on CH–47D's? It's an older plane, I understand, but should we get a black box on them in the future?

Mr. REID. I'm aware that the newer—I'm not an aviator, but I'm aware of the newer platforms, as the digital platforms are fielded, that that is a standard configuration. I've also told that it's not technically possible for the analog aircraft to replicate that.

Mrs. MALONEY. Okay. Thank you very much.

Mr. CHAFFETZ. Thank you. I'll now recognize the gentleman from Florida, Mr. Mica, for 5 minutes.

Mr. MICA. Thank you, Mr. Chairman.

Mr. Reid, this is one of the greatest losses of life that we have had in any single incident. I guess that's correct?

Mr. REID. This is the largest loss in Afghanistan, sir, that's correct.

Mr. MICA. Okay. What was used? Was it an MH–47, or is there a difference between a CH–47D or Chinook helicopter? What was used?

Mr. REID. The aircraft, Extortion 17, was a model of Chinook, the D model, the delta model, CH–47.

Mr. MICA. And this was a high risk mission?

Mr. REID. The risk assessment for the mission profile overall as a commander's risk assessment was a high risk mission, yes, sir.

Mr. MICA. And we put our—our men in equipment that couldn't be protected. I chaired aviation. We developed—we have equipment for commercial airliners that's available. We have—I've been in Afghanistan. They only put me on certain types of flight equipment that would protect me, particularly from RPG's.

Why would we risk our—a high risk mission on—putting our men on this kind of equipment? See, first I want to—I'm already concerned you put our people at risk on equipment, and we know we have equipment for a high risk mission where they wouldn't be put at risk or killed. We do have that equipment, don't we, sir?

Mr. REID. Sir, specific to this, no.

Mr. MICA. We do not have equipment in Afghanistan that would have allowed some protection against RPG fire, you're telling me and this committee?

Mr. REID. For this particular, yes, sir, that's correct.

Mr. MICA. Okay. And this was a high risk mission. Now, you also testified that those guys, or whoever fired this, were in some building. I'm very concerned about the people that were in that building. Don't we assess the risk, and you just said it was a high risk mission, that these guys are there?

I don't know if we can discuss the investigation, the post investigation about the Afghans and how much information they had about the mission, and if that mission placed those people in a position where they can use those RPG's to take down a piece of equipment that couldn't protect our people. Now, was there a thorough investigation, in your opinion? In August 6th, 2011, were you there, were you in charge of this mission?

Mr. REID. No, sir. I am a civilian——

Mr. MICA. Okay. Who was in charge of the mission?

Mr. REID. U.S. Central Command, sir.

Mr. MICA. But who was the individual in charge? I think we need to be hearing from that individual. I'd like to also find out who made the decision. Also, I want to know about the investigation and who was investigation—what Afghans had information as to this mission.

Mr. REID. Sir, no Afghans were provided information on the mission. The eight Afghans onboard were part of our team.

Mr. MICA. And none of the Afghans were briefed in advance as to where they were going?

Mr. REID. Not outside that team, sir, no.

Mr. MICA. Again, I would like to see further reports and I'd like it made part of a reference to—and if it is classified information. But I'm very concerned, one, the right equipment wasn't used, we put our people at risk, and also we pass—I just do not trust the Afghanis. When I was there, I'm telling you, they—they're—they're—everything they do I would question, right from the president, who I think is corrupt, and the money that we're pouring down that rat hole and then losing lives on top of this is sinful.

But, Mr. Brown, Army Mortuary, is the mess at Arlington cleaned up in the way we treat our—the remains of our fallen? Are you satisfied with what has been done there? I've never seen anything so disgusting as the mess, the misplacement, the mistreatment, the use of human remains of our servicemen and women as what I've learned took place at Arlington. Is that mess cleaned up? Have you followed that?

Colonel BROWN. Sir, that is outside my purview.

Mr. MICA. How long have you been there, and how long have you been in this particular position?

Colonel BROWN. Sir, I have served as a director of Army Casualty since July of 2012.

Mr. MICA. Well, again, you are aware of the mess I am talking about?

Colonel BROWN. Yes, sir, I am.

Mr. MICA. Okay. And can you provide me the names of the individuals and put it in the record of who was in charge of the remains at that particular time. And then I would like a statement from you or from someone in your office that you believe that the situation has been cleared up, that the remains that were misplaced or abused, that we have also taken care of that situation. Can you provide that to the committee?

Colonel BROWN. Sir, I will provide that for the record.

Mr. MICA. Thank you.

I yield back.

Mr. CHAFFETZ. I now recognize the gentleman from Massachusetts, Mr. Lynch, for 5 minutes.

Mr. LYNCH. Thank you, Mr. Chairman.

Along with the other members, I want to offer my condolences to all the families of our fallen heros. We are deeply appreciative of all of their family service and sacrifice.

I do, as a threshold matter, I want to acknowledge Mr. Chairman and our ranking member, Mr. Tierney, the work that you have done on this and both staffs, Democrat and Republican, working together, the energy and thoroughness with which the committee has taken great pains and sensitivity regarding the families involved and the issues involved. This is the way government is supposed to work, side by side.

Mr. Reid, I want to ask you about this CH–47D Chinook. You know, I have been to Afghanistan nine times. I spent a lot of time, you know, in contrast to the earlier gentleman's comments that we never put, you know, people that we value on a CH–47, I have spent a lot of time on that aircraft. So maybe they just don't value me so much. I don't know, but I have spent a fair amount of time. And I have also talked to the pilots and crew, mechanics about— and they love this aircraft, the CH–47D. They say they can perform simple maintenance. It is a very reliable aircraft, but there have been a lot of questions in the general press about the appropriateness of using the CH–47D, the Chinook, in this instance, knowing the topography of the Tangi Valley, very tight, mountains on the northern end there. It widens out in the south.

But given the aggregate circumstances here, was this an appropriate aircraft to use, or was this something that was thrown together at the last minute, because that allegation has been out there as well?

Mr. REID. Thank you, sir. This was the appropriate aircraft for this mission. The choice of this aircraft was tactically sound. Other aircraft may have been used, but what could not have been used and has been questioned was the Black Hawk. One of the issues with the war in Afghanistan is the elevation in the mountains, and the Chinook helicopter, which, frankly, in my career, we did not use extensively in other conflicts, and even in Iraq, the first time or the second time, you see mostly Black Hawks. That is a function of the elevation.

The Chinook—D Model Chinook is the same engines as the Special Operations model. The distinction of the Special Operations models is the high technology, terrain-following navigation system, and the in-flight refueling capability and the larger fuel tanks. Beyond that, they are essentially the same aircraft. What that means is, for certain mission profiles, you must use the MH47. This particular tactical mission was about a 15-mile flight on known terrain in clear weather. The avionics capabilities of the MH47 were not necessary to conduct this mission.

Both aircraft have the identical survivability. And if I may clarify, sir, there is no active technology countermeasure to defeat the RPG. The RPG is a rocket-propelled grenade. I believe what the gentleman was referring to were for surface-to-air missiles that have a radar signature or an active seeker. We have countermeasures for those. We do not have countermeasures for a ballistic rocket-propelled grenade right now active. We are researching and trying to do that, and none currently exists.

Mr. LYNCH. I appreciate that. Let me ask you, the other criticism that has been out there in the press is that the way this went down, that there was a several-hour fire fight, that there were a number of helos in the area, Apaches and also the Ranger team that went in first. And then, when the Chinook came in with 30 personnel on board, that it was, you know, tactically inadvisable to have a long-term fire fight making the insurgents in that area aware of a major operation and then having the Chinook come in, you know, a relatively slower aircraft and then being exposed to insurgent fire. Can you address those allegations?

Mr. REID. Yes, sir. Thank you. The investigating officer did conclude that the presence of our activity in that valley likely put the enemy on a heightened state of alert. That is true. The tactical planning and the commanders' decisions to mitigate against that were to approach from the opposite direction at a low altitude.

The area was scanned by our overhead platforms. The C130 had overview of the whole battlefield, the Apaches air weapons team scanned the LZ 1 minute prior, confirmed no enemy presence on the LZ. The enemy that fired at Extortion 17 remained undetected through those scans. We did not detect that enemy, and we did not achieve, frankly, the element of surprise into the Valley that was planned and anticipated.

Mr. LYNCH. Okay. I believe my time is expired.

I thank the Chairman. I yield back.

Mr. CHAFFETZ. I now recognize the gentlewoman from California, Ms. Speier.

Ms. SPEIER. Mr. Chairman, thank you, and thank you to all of the members of the panel. And let me first say to the families who are here, we know how broken your hearts are. And we share, albeit at some distance, the same sense of loss that you do. And there is no way that we can make you whole again, and that is very difficult, I think, for all of us. And hopefully, through this hearing and others, we will at least have solace in knowing that we will take steps to make sure that those who are serving our country in war zones have absolutely the best protection available.

We can't foresee everything. That is why we have lost the men and women in battle that we have, but that doesn't mean we shouldn't redouble our efforts to try and protect them, so thank you.

Let me ask, there have been concerns raised about the way those fallen service members from Extortion 17 were transported and whether they were accorded the appropriate respect. For instance, some have raised concerns about which flags were used to drape over the caskets of some of the fallen heros during a ceremony at Bagram Airfield and again at the Dignified Transfer Ceremony at Dover.

Colonel, could you provide for us an understanding about the catastrophic nature of this crash that, from what I understand, made it impossible in some respects to distinguish Americans from Afghan dead. The identities of the remains of Extortion 17 service members were not known until after they were examined, my understanding is, by the medical examiner in Dover following the transfer ceremony. Is that right?

Colonel DEVILLIER. Thank you, ma'am, for your question. That is correct. Given the trauma associated with this incident, all of the remains were brought to Dover as believed to be unknown, and until scientifically identified by the Armed Forces Medical Examiner, there was no way to positively identify these individuals.

Ms. SPEIER. Is that the protocol that is always used and has always been used historically?

Colonel DEVILLIER. Yes, ma'am, until they are scientifically identified by the Armed Forces Medical Examiner, every remain that comes to Dover is believed to be—they can be visually recognized in certain instances, so every situation is different. This particular situation was an aircraft accident. It was very traumatic.

Ms. SPEIER. In hindsight, would you have handled it any differently?

Colonel DEVILLIER. Well, ma'am, you know, the decisions were made at the time based upon the information they had available. And the scientific identification process has to occur at Dover Air Force.

Ms. SPEIER. I understand that. I am just trying to put myself in the shoes of family members who were at the ceremony watching these caskets come off without an American flag draped over them. And, I mean, arguably maybe you would have the Afghan flag and the American flag. I don't know what the right answer is, but having a coffin come off that has no flag draped on it, I am sure gave the family members a sense of pain that was magnified by everything else that they had endured.

Colonel DEVILLIER. Ma'am, while I was not there at the time of the event, I can tell you that there was a lot of debate that occurred about this on how to properly provide dignity, honor and respect to all of the members of Extortion 17. And there were different courses of action that were discussed with the leadership within the Office of Secretary of Defense. And their final determination was to flag drape 30 of the transfer cases with American flags and 8 with the Afghan flags.

Ms. SPEIER. And that decision was based on what?

Ms. SKILLMAN. Ma'am, if I may respond to that question, again, as Colonel Devillier had stated our leadership was presented with several courses of action after we had discussed with our colleagues within the Service Casualty Department of how to best honor our military service members, the U.S. fallen, and also our coalition forces, understanding that remains were en route to the United States, we had to make a decision rather quickly. Again, it was a catastrophic event, largest incident of—number of fallen in one single incident in Afghanistan. So, based off the courses of action consult with our military departments, OSD leadership decided that to best honor, we would be able to display the 30 transfer cases as best we could identify were carrying our U.S. service members and 8, our coalition forces.

I would also emphasize that in transport to the United States, all remains were under U.S. flag cover, as per our policy if we cannot make the distinction. So, en route on the aircraft, all 38 transfer cases were under U.S. flag cover.

Ms. SPEIER. I realize my time is expired, Mr. Chairman, if you would just indulge me for one moment. I think it would just be helpful to all of us if you queried the family members as to how they perceived the return and if they had any, would have any suggestions, just for future reference.

I yield back.

Mr. CHAFFETZ. Thank you. I will new recognize the gentlewoman from Illinois, Ms. Kelly, for 5 minutes.

Ms. KELLY. Thank you, Mr. Chair.

I want to thank the witnesses for being here, and thank you for your service to our country and to all the Service folks in the audience, whether retired or not, and my condolences to the family.

Ms. Skillman, you spoke about the person authorized to direct disposition. And I was just curious, is there special resources or tools that are given to the families or there for the families to help them through this time or whoever the person is that has been appointed the PADD? Do you help them with their decision or——

Ms. SKILLMAN. Ma'am, a casualty assistance officer—and each of the service departments call their assistance officers different names, but we will refer to them as assistance officers—are assigned to the designated person, the PADD. And they are provided information. We do not persuade. We don't make recommendations. We merely try to make sure that they have all the information available to them to help them in making a decision. They are provided with the options that are available to them and the amounts that are allowable under law to pay for any funeral expenses and what the government can provide for them.

Ms. KELLY. Thank you, and I yield back.

Mr. CHAFFETZ. Thank you.

Pursuant to committee rules, members of the committee—my apologies. I now recognize the gentleman from Vermont, Mr. Welch, for 5 minutes.

Mr. WELCH. Thank you very much.

I thank Mr. Chaffetz and Mr. Tierney for the hearing, and I want to thank very much Mr. Rigell for being here, since he represents so many of the soldiers who died in service to their country.

Thank you very much. And I want to thank the families, and I want to thank you.

How can any of us deal with the loss of a loved one? We are all proud obviously of those who die in service of our country. Our responsibility is to recognize that we have these Americans who sign up and volunteer, no matter what the mission may be. And they will report for duty when the commander in chief says, We need you. This democracy would never work if we didn't have citizens who were willing to put aside their own judgment when it comes to what America's engagement should be and defer to civilian leadership. And our responsibility here more than anything else is to make certain that the missions that we set America on are worthy of the willingness of our civilians who become military people to make the ultimate sacrifice. So I say that really out of respect to the families.

And I am going to ask one question that I know the answer to. These families have all been affected in the same way. They have lost a loved one, but they have all been affected in different ways because how one deals with loss is very personal. And some people need more information; some people need more privacy. And the question I have of you is will you be available to each of the families to give them every bit of information that you can about every detail that they seek to try to respect the needs and desires and the emotions of each of the families? And they have different ways of trying to work through this enormous loss. Thank you.

Ms. SKILLMAN. Yes, sir. I think I can speak on behalf of all of my colleagues here. We welcome the opportunity to assist every family member with their individual needs, and we will be more than happy to speak to the family members when they are ready.

Mr. CHAFFETZ. Thank the gentlemen.

Pursuant to committee rules, we do have some flexibility in allowing colleagues who do not serve on this committee to join us and ask questions. I would ask my colleagues for unanimous consent to allow Mr. Rigell of Virginia and Mr. Fortenberry to ask—each be granted 5 minutes to ask questions.

Mr. TIERNEY. Without objection.

Mr. CHAFFETZ. Without objection, so ordered.

They care deeply about this issue. I appreciate their participation and serve on committees that are also very relevant to this issue, so I appreciate their presence.

I now recognize Mr. Rigell for 5 minutes.

Mr. RIGELL. Well, given that I do not serve on this committee, I am especially grateful to the chairman and to all members for the unanimous consent that was required.

And the title of the hearing is, ''Honoring the Heros of Extortion 17,'' and my comments are provided here today in that spirit, and I hope it honors the good men that we lost.

Even within a community that accepts the great risk that comes with our mission, the loss of Extortion 17 was truly tragic and profound. And so to the families that are here today, from one American to another, I offer you my deepest condolences.

Now, the tragedy merits and should receive, and I believe has received, rigorous examination, unflinching examination, looking at each and every measure to see if, indeed, we could have done something different, because we owe that to the men who we lost that day to honor their memory. And also we owe it to the commanders and the warfighters that will follow them to provide that with any lessons that could be learned to give our warfighter every advantage in equipment, tactical procedures, and doctrine to allow them to come home safe.

You know, each member of this body has standing here, whether a member lost someone in their district or not, that, as my friend and colleague, Mr. Welch, I think gracefully offered, our district has had a disproportionate loss. And it is both humbling and honoring to me and sobering really to represent so many of our warfighters and their families.

It is well known, I think, that there is at least some degree of controversy associated with the hearing itself. There is not unanimity among the family members, and I have a duty and the privilege of representing the Second District in Virginia, and the families who are there overwhelmingly have made clear that their desire would be that we did not hold the hearing. But I am especially grateful to the chairman and to all who have offered their remarks today that there is a deep level of respect, and our heartfelt condolences extend, of course, to each and every family.

I have listened carefully to the testimony that has been offered here today. It is under oath. Each one of you, I believe, meets the highest standard of an American patriot, and it is not a term that I offer casually. I deeply respect your service to our country.

Mr. Reid, I think your own experience in particular and your intense investigation here is noteworthy. Do you have any question whatsoever, Mr. Reid, that there was no communication at all between Americans and Afghans that would have in any way jeopardized or compromised that mission?

Mr. REID. No, sir, I do not have any questions that that information was provided. I know from those involved that this particular 17 mission was not coordinated externally.

Mr. RIGELL. Is it your testimony here today that the aircraft that was selected for this operation was appropriate to the mission?

Mr. REID. Yes sir.

Mr. RIGELL. The testimony that I have heard, not only today but the classified material itself, which of course we cannot go into, I do, and this is with deep respect for those who actually hold a different view, I find compelling. And I would hope that in this hearing, the fact that it was held, that it can bring just perhaps a measure of closure on some of the technical issues that need to have been worked through and I think, indeed, have.

It is certainly to my satisfaction, so I thank all who are here today. I certainly thank all who have testified. I thank the chairman and all the members of the committee for the opportunity to speak.

And I yield back the remainder of my time.

Mr. CHAFFETZ. Thank the gentleman.

I now recognize the gentleman from Nebraska, Mr. Fortenberry, for 5 minutes.

Mr. FORTENBERRY. Thank you, Chairman Chaffetz, for extending me the courtesy of being able to speak here and members of the committee as well. I am grateful for the opportunity to participate in this difficult moment for many of the families here but those of you as well who attend to these families. This is difficult for all of us.

And first, let me extend my heartfelt sympathies to all who have lost loved ones through this tragic incident and also commend Mr. Rigell for something that I think he put very well. I hope that the outcome of this committee provides some measure of closure for all of those who have suffered so grievously.

In late summer of 2011, my office, I was notified that a young man from South Sioux City, Nebraska, had been killed. His name was John Douangdara. John was a first generation American. His parents had fled Communism in Laos and come to the United States in 1975 to rebuild their lives. They are good Americans. And their son, after high school, like so many other Americans, right after 9/11, joined the Navy. This was his fifth tour your of duty, and John had a specialty. He had an assault dog, a specialty with an assault dog, whose name was Bart, who happened to be on this helicopter as well and was also killed.

The family was kind enough to ask me to speak at the memorial service there in South Sioux City and then kind enough again, even though this is no longer in my congressional district because the lines have changed, to invite me back on Memorial Day last year for the unveiling of a statute of John and his dog Bart at the park there in South Sioux City.

Now, those of you who are in the military and those of you who have lost a loved one, to know that all of your loved ones are honored in a particular special way but to know John's story as well and to have seen what I saw, the outpouring of support from that little, small community there along the Missouri River, called South Sioux City, should be uplifting to all of us as Americans.

I did only have one brief question, and it is a sensitive issue, but I would like to get a little bit more clarity on it. You mentioned the memorial service that took place immediately after the incident. Were there insulting remarks made by an Afghan cleric there?

Mr. REID. Thank you, Congressman.

Three people spoke at the ceremony that you are asking about. It is a memorial service; the troops call it a ramp ceremony. We make a distinction in policy between ceremonies and services, but they call it a ramp ceremony. And they have been doing them the whole war. And it is an important—and if I may, I will get to that. The question was asked earlier about why we do that. The troops are in the battlefield, and they are continuing the fight. They don't come back to see their loved comrades off, so that is their farewell.

They are filmed, and they are filmed for the purpose of providing those to the families. They are filmed by that organization at the commander's discretion at that time within policy. As you heard the policy has been changed by CENTCOM in 2013. But they are done so for the families, and they provide that to them as a memento of what they did down range.

Three people spoke, the commander of our Special Operations Task Force, a U.S. military chaplain, and the third gentleman, to get to your question, is an Afghan. He is a colonel. He is a commander of the Afghan unit that we work with. He has been working with us in a very trusted, close and cooperative way for several years. I believe now—he is still there; started, I believe, in 2009. He accounts for those special troops that are assigned to our task force. And as I mentioned, they come out of the other forces. We run a special selection and a vetting and a training program for them. He is the one that spoke. There is no other one that spoke.

I don't speak Arabic. I am not a religious scholar. We have had people in our government listen to what he was saying. I am told—again, not my authority—that there are verses that he is citing. He is commemorating the fallen, all of the fallen. There are some interpretations I have seen on the internet that he is condemning the Americans, the infidels. Again, it is not my expertise, but what we have been told on good authority is he is commemorating all of our fallen and condemning the enemy. But I understand things are subject to interpretation, sir. That is who was speaking.

Mr. FORTENBERRY. And that was one of the points that I think was particularly sensitive that was under public scrutiny about the entire incident.

Mr. Chairman, thank you for the privilege of being with you during this particularly difficult hearing.

Let me just conclude that I am not here on behalf of the Douangdara family. I just got to know them, and I wanted in some small measure to honor John's life. He was dedicated to his community. He was a warrior. John was an American.

Mr. CHAFFETZ. Thank the gentleman.

I thank both of you for your participation and your heart and caring.

We will now recognize the gentlewoman from New Mexico, Ms. Lujan Grisham, for 5 minutes.

Ms. LUJAN GRISHAM. Thank you, Mr. Chairman.

And I, too, very much appreciate your participation in today's hearing and to work diligently to assure that we have the right protocols and procedures to support the men and women who give their lives and their families in the most appropriate, meaningful way that we possibly can. I cannot imagine the pain of losing a family member or a loved one in this kind of an incident. And I offer and share with my colleagues in giving my deepest condolences and sympathies for the family members who are here today and all those family members who have suffered these kinds of losses on behalf of this country.

And I also agree that the Department of Defense has an obligation to do absolutely everything that it possibly can do to be open, transparent, comforting, supportive, and to do that at the highest possible level to the family members and every family member who has suffered through the loss of a loved one. So I know that you have been doing this, and I want you to keep doing it.

Walk me through the process and the protocol that the DOD has in place now to ensure that there is direct and a sustained line of communication between the Department of Defense Family Liaison Offices and the family members of Americans serving in harm's way, and what services and supports specifically are you providing?

Ms. SKILLMAN. Ma'am, thank you for your question. If I understand your question, the level of support that we are providing, the continued support that we provide to our surviving family members?

Ms. LUJAN GRISHAM. Correct.

Ms. SKILLMAN. Our current policy requires, of course, that an assistance officer, whether it is a casualty assistance representative from the Air Force or a casualty assistance officer from the Army or a casualty assistance calls officer from Navy or Marine Corps, assist the family members through the initial phase of the loss. We are also required to provide long-term support for those family members for as long as they want to be part of the military community. Again, we want that family member to feel that they can be part of the military community for as long as they need us.

Each Service has their own long-term care program. Army, for example, can expound upon that. They have a Survivor OutReach Services Program, and I will allow each of the Services just to talk about their program, but that program is in place where there are people that are available for the family members to contact to provide that long-term care support.

Ms. LUJAN GRISHAM. Thank you. Can you give me some specifics. So that is going to be counseling? Are there therapeutic services, an opportunity for suggestions about how to improve those processes, involvement in the services to the highest degree possible? Can you give me some level of specificity about the kinds of services that you are providing to family members and loved ones?

Ms. SKILLMAN. Yes, ma'am. Each of those long-term programs, they want to keep them involved, especially around their community. Some family members are not close to a military installation, so we want to reach out to them, make sure that they are part of the community. TAPS is an integral part of that. We constantly work with our other agencies that provide support to our family members, so the Marine Corps may invite family members to TAPS events. The Army Survivor Outreach Services may bring in—provide a session that provides some counseling for family members; make sure that if they need bereavement counseling, they can reach out to the Department of Veterans Affairs or other agencies who may be providing that level of support. But again, it is a case manager that is assigned to that family member that knows what their specific needs are.

Ms. LUJAN GRISHAM. And given that each one of these tragedies is very difficult to accept, we want to absolutely evaluate it in the context of mitigating for the future but also supporting men and women and, again, the family members who suffer these kinds of tragedies, is there a process also for being clear about things that the families want you to do to improve and how that communication occurs? And what can Congress be doing to ensure that all of these protocols and all of these processes continue to sort of amend and grow and really meet the needs of both the current situations and the potential for future issues that should be supported in the context of these families?

Ms. SKILLMAN. Thank you, ma'am.

Our current program requires that we proactively provide family members and inform them of specific Federal entitlements. That long-term program, of course, is dependent upon the family's needs. We have two governing bodies, the Casualty Advisory Board and the Central Joint Mortuary Affairs Board that meets quarterly. Those two boards that these members represent, they are voting members on both of those boards, as I know OSD chairs both of them. They are the governing bodies that we ensure that we are doing things right by the family members. At those times, we review specific cases. We may review our policies, make recommendations where we think legislation needs to be corrected. Where a survivor's needs are not being met, there may be a gap in law or policy. And those boards, we make those recommendations at that time.

Ms. LUJAN GRISHAM. And, Mr. Chairman, with your diligence, I have one small follow up.

And how often are those reports or suggestions, is that annually? Do you do it quarterly, and I would suggest that we have more access to that kind of information in this committee, Mr. Chairman.

Ms. SKILLMAN. Ma'am, we meet quarterly.

Ms. LUJAN GRISHAM. But that information is available quarterly, or do you do kind of an annual report?

Ms. SKILLMAN. There is no reporting requirement to Congress at this time, ma'am.

Ms. LUJAN GRISHAM. Thank you, Mr. Chairman.

I yield back.

Mr. CHAFFETZ. In consultation with the Ranking Member Tierney, I have a series of questions. We tried to get as many different questions from the families as possible, so I am going to go through a series of questions here. Again, it won't answer every question that every family member has, but I think it is a good representation of some of their specific concerns.

First of all, I can tell you that having reviewed the records, the pilots that were operating this aircraft are of exceptional quality, skill and high rating, but there were some questions about why was there no pre-assault fire laid down before, as this helicopter was coming in. Could you help clarify that, Mr. Reid?

Mr. REID. Yes, sir. Thank you. The use of pre-assault fire is a tactical decision based on conditions on the ground. The objective of Extortion 17 was to get into the LZ and drop off the assault force and depart the area without alerting the enemy overtly. I think as we explained to you the other day, the force was going to then walk closer to the target. So you are trying to achieve surprise. Firing in advance of that in a suppressive fire mode would be highly alerting to the enemy, and, secondly, there was no enemy detected on the landing zone. But let me just clarify, this is a tactical decision.

Mr. CHAFFETZ. Can you give us a general sense of the time of day that this is happening?

Mr. REID. 2:39 in the morning on the morning of August 6, 2011.

Mr. CHAFFETZ. One of the concerns and the questions about the Afghans that were on this helicopter, there were some allegations that there were Afghans on the helicopter, I should say, and then got off, and a different group got on, which begs an awful lot of questions. Can you help clarify that, please?

Mr. REID. Yes, sir. Thank you. There are two groups of Afghans assigned to this task force. One group went on the first Target with the Rangers. The second group was on Extortion 17. There was a mistake made after the crash to retrieve the list of Afghans that were aboard 17. The list that was provided was for the other squad that was with the Rangers. This created this confusion and led to some speculation that there was a switching out of the actual forces. That is not the case, sir.

Mr. CHAFFETZ. Why were there Afghans on the plane, and what kind of experience did we have with these people—I keep saying plane. On the helicopter. What kind of experience did we have? How many times, missions, had they done in the past? Was this a new group. Can you provide some context there, please?

Mr. REID. Yes, sir. This group of Afghans we referred to as our partnered unit, and they have been aligned with our assault forces going back to 2009. The purpose of these forces is to facilitate actions on the objective, primarily by speaking with and dealing with the enemy and the civilians on the target because they speak the language and they know the culture.

As was mentioned earlier, the majority of these missions since we started doing this result in what we call a tactical callout, saying we are out here, come out. And 80 percent of the missions, therefore, because of this capability are accomplished without any shots being fired. So it greatly enhances our safety. That is why they were there. How they got there is through a very long and extensive training cycle that lasts about 7 months. They are hand selected out of the Afghan Army and Afghan police and their other security services. They are vetted, trained and selected, and then aligned with our units. They are paired with our forces. They go on a rotation cycle, just like our forces did. Our assault forces come in for about 90 days in cycles, and we rotate them back out. We align the Afghans in a similar cycle, and they repeat that. These folks, again, for the previous 2 years prior to this, every mission we are taking them on the objective with us. This was not a new construct.

Mr. CHAFFETZ. My understanding is that General Colt conducted part of this review, and one of the questions is why it appears there were no Afghans that were interviewed. Why not?

Mr. REID. Sir, I don't know specifically why no Afghans were interviewed. The focus of his investigation and the list of questions that the commander of CENTCOM charged him to answer did not require him to interview others outside our decision chain and our training and equipment chain.

Mr. CHAFFETZ. Perhaps you can provide some additional clarification for the committee. That would be appreciated. I want to go back to the ramp ceremony itself. Having been through a number of meetings, classified, unclassified discussions, not to belabor the point, but to my colleagues here, I think one of the—and this is just Jason Chaffetz, just me personally, my personal take on it. You all are the experts. You have been doing this for years, but my sense of it is that if you do have a situation where there are deceased Americans and whatever country, in this case Afghanistan, my sense of it is that there probably should be two different ceremonies.

I think if—I mean, I can't even imagine having my son or daughter go through this, but I don't want some Afghan saying something about my son. I don't want that. So I hope—we are supposed to be the Oversight and Government Reform. I would hope the Pentagon would seriously consider—honoring those Americans is our number one priority, and of course, we are going to honor those that also lost their lives, but do it separately. And let's not have this mistake and this heartache that these families feel. That is my suggestion.

And, Ms. Skillman, I need you or one of the others to help explain, clarify, just how is it we can lay a tombstone and then have to go back and change it. And in some cases, I think it happened three times. Can you shed some light on this? You are a very committed, patriotic person. It is not all on her shoulders.

To the families and members here, she is the brave one who is sitting here helping us.

But this is very hard for a family to go through. Can you please shed some light on this?

Ms. SKILLMAN. Yes, sir. The group internment, I believe, is what you are referring to here, is that group headstone that is at Arlington National Cemetery. Per our current policy, we may decide if there are remains that cannot be identified to a single individual, that we may have a group internment of those at a specific place. Arlington is picked pretty regularly, and then a headstone is placed on that location.

Normally we list the names of the deceased. There are some challenges in this particular case because of our coalition forces, and we struggled with how we would appropriately label that headstone. And in deference to the family members, we should have given them the opportunity to review our suggestions. And I think that is something that we can look at before we ever put another headstone on a group internment, conferring with the family members of how they would like that to be done.

Mr. CHAFFETZ. I appreciate that, and I have one more topic and then if any members have additional questions.

You know, the people out there who are paying attention and care about Extortion 17, they didn't just make this thing up about a black box being washed away. That wasn't just something that somebody made up out of the blue. There is some reason to believe that the, I am not sure what his rank is, but the commander essentially on the ground, made note of the fact that they were looking for in black box and they couldn't find the black box.

Again, you are telling us, Mr. Reid, that these helicopters aren't even equipped with them, but how is it the commander wouldn't know that.

Mr. REID. Sir, I can't speak exactly for what the commander thought. I have seen the transcript of where he talked about looking for it. I would say, though, that this crash environment is a hostile environment. We did not have complete freedom of action, freedom of thought of what we were doing, what we were coordinating and what we were looking for. That team went in there in the immediate moments after the crash to recover the fallen, as I indicated, over a period of 4 days going through the wreckage. I don't know why they thought they would be looking for one either, but I have spoken to our aviation community. And they have assured me that those helicopters are not equipped with such a device.

Mr. CHAFFETZ. Thank you, and for those on the committee, I just want people to know that many of our men and women who are intimately involved in this are also continuing to serve and serve abroad.

Anyway, I appreciate it. Does any other member have additional question or comment?

Gentlewoman from Wyoming.

Mrs. LUMMIS. Mr. Chairman, I simply want to comment that I am proud of the work you have done as chairman, on this. It is apparent that you went through this record exhaustively and that you took to heart the concerns that certain family members have.

I recognize that there are other families who may have felt differently about the appropriateness of this hearing, but I just want to commend you and thank you for your diligent regard for the families who did have concerns so they would have an opportunity today to hear you ask the questions that they have had on their minds and hearts.

And I just want to thank you, Mr. Chairman. I think you have done a very commendable thing.

Mr. CHAFFETZ. Thank you.

We recognize the gentleman from Massachusetts, Mr. Tierney.

Mr. TIERNEY. Thank you.

Well, I just want to add my comments that I hope the families that have had concerns and questions have now felt that they have had an opportunity to hear fairly broadly answers to those concerns and that they are going to be heard going forward and attention will be paid to their continuing concerns and questions.

But I want to address our panelists here today. I think nothing that I have read or heard would indicate that any of you proceeded or any of those under your commands have proceeded with anything but the best of intentions and caring and concern for their colleagues with whom they either work directly or indirectly or at least emphasize with because of their shared commitment to this country and to each other. And I commend all of you also for diligently going about your investigations and your review in the same manner and also the willingness to learn where learning is appropriate on that.

And thank you for your service and for the way that you have represented your country well.

Mr. CHAFFETZ. Thank you.

As we conclude here, I want to first thank the five people that are sitting here before us. You have a tough assignment but probably one of the most important assignments. It is a great opportunity, and I know you all feel that. I have chatted with you previously. I can tell that in your demeanor and your approach. We thank you for your service and your dedication.

Most importantly, we obviously unanimously, regardless of party or politics or anything else, we cannot thank the men and women enough who serve this Nation and those that have given their lives for this Nation.

There is a different group of people in our country, and these are the men and women who run to action. They run to the fire fight. That is the American way. There is a certain group of people who just do that. They just do it instinctively, and those Americans who do that are my heroes. I thank the families for their sacrifice. That is quite a thing that this is the largest loss of life, but it has happened unfortunately thousands of times. And I just hope they feel the love of this Nation, and so I appreciate the hearing. We stand adjourned.

[Whereupon, at 11:47 a.m., the subcommittee was adjourned.]

APPENDIX

MATERIAL SUBMITTED FOR THE HEARING RECORD

Joint Statement For
OSD, Army & Navy
Casualty & Mortuary Affairs

BEFORE THE

NATIONAL SECURITY SUBCOMMITTEE
HOUSE OVERSIGHT AND GOVERNMENT REFORM COMMITTEE

SECOND SESSION, 113TH CONGRESS

EXTORTION 17

FEBRUARY 27, 2014

The Department holds casualty and mortuary affairs among its most solemn responsibilities to our Service members, surviving family members, and the nation. A fundamental element of military culture and tradition is that we hold our fallen in highest esteem, treat their remains with highest reverence, and provide their surviving family members the highest level of care and continued support. The Office of Casualty and Mortuary Affairs promulgates policies that reflect these core values, and works in coordination with the Military Departments and the Services to ensure that the intent of the policies is reflected throughout all casualty and mortuary tasks and processes.

Casualty Assistance:

The Secretary of Defense is responsible for establishing uniform personnel policies and procedures for reporting, recording, notifying, and assisting the next of kin of Service members who are deceased, duty status - whereabouts unknown (DUSTWUN), excused absence – whereabouts unknown (EAWUN), missing, ill, or injured. The Office of the secretary of Defense (OSD) also establishes uniform policy and procedures for reporting, recording, notifying, and assisting the next of kin of DoD civilian personnel, eligible contractors, and other designated or covered personnel. These policies apply to the Military Departments, Joint Staff, Combatant Commands, Office of the Inspector General of the Department of Defense, Defense Agencies, DoD Field Activities, and all other organizational entities in the Department of Defense. To carry out this mission, DoD has established procedures for completing and updating the Record of Emergency Data or DD Form 93. The DD Form 93 is an official record for military personnel that provides the names and addresses of the persons the Service member desires to be notified in case of injury or death, designates certain benefits in the event of a Service members' death, and designates the person authorized to direct disposition of his or her remains. The DD Form 93 also serves as a guide for the disposition of pay and allowances if captured, missing, or deceased. This form is also used for civilian personnel as emergency notification in the event the civilian member becomes a casualty.

Mortuary Affairs:

In addition to providing policy oversight for casualty assistance, the Office of Casualty and Mortuary Affairs provides overarching policy guidance and serves as the Department's focal point for coordination of all matters related to the DoD Mortuary Affairs Program. This includes policy oversight for the handling and transportation of human remains; group interments, disinterments, memorial ceremonies, and cremation of remains.

Program Governance and Oversight:

DoD has codified the Departments' policies in Department of Defense Directive 1300.22E, Mortuary Affairs Policy, and Department of Defense Instruction 1300.18, Personnel Casualty Matters, Policies, and Procedures which are further augmented by Service specific instructions, regulations or directives. DoD meets the statutory requirement as described in Section 562 of Public Law 109-163, to provide a uniformed casualty assistance program by defining the core training requirements for all casualty assistance personnel regardless of Service. The Services then establish additional requirements to address the Service-unique circumstances of their members, families, organizational structure and traditions. To ensure DoD is meeting the needs of our Service members and their families, and to ensure uniformity with DoD casualty and mortuary affairs polices, the Department established the Central Joint Mortuary Affairs Board and the Casualty Advisory Board as governing bodies for all matters relating to mortuary affairs and casualty assistance policies respectively. These Boards meet quarterly with representatives from all Services, the Department of Veterans Affairs, the Armed Forces Medical Examiner, and other agencies to discuss casualty and mortuary policies and procedures. In addition to these boards, OSD conducts a monthly survey of DoD survivors, and the Director, Casualty and Mortuary Affairs serves as a co-chair on the DoD and Department of Veterans Affairs Survivors' Forum. The Service specific operations and procedures are provided in more detail throughout the remainder of this written statement.

Army Casualty Overview

The Army has been in a state of continuous war for over twelve years -- the longest in our Nation's history. More than 4,900 Soldiers have given their lives on behalf of this Nation. Behind each and every one of these Soldiers is a Survivor or Survivors, and it is the Army's charter to provide the best support possible to ease their transitions. The mission of the Casualty and Mortuary Affairs Operations Center is to execute the full-spectrum of Army Casualty and Mortuary Affairs for present and past conflicts. In this role, the Casualty and Mortuary Affairs Operations Center provides policy and direction to 33 Casualty Assistance Centers, develops standardized Casualty Assistance and Casualty Notification Officer training, operates the Joint Personal Effects Depot where Personal Effects for deceased personnel for all Service members who die in the combat theater of operations are processed/cleaned and returned to family or loved ones and provides notification, casualty assistance, and case management for injured, ill, missing and deceased personnel. Casualty notification and initial support are completed through Casualty Notification Officers and Casualty Assistance Officers.

Army Casualty Notification Officer

The Casualty Notification Officer (CNO) represents the Secretary of the Army. The notification officer is courteous, helpful and compassionate toward the Next of Kin and reflects the Army's concern for its personnel and their families while performing this sensitive and honorable mission. Trained active duty officers in the rank of captain and higher, warrant officers in the rank of chief warrant officer two and higher, and senior noncommissioned officers in the rank of sergeant first class and higher, are charged with personally notifying the Next of Kin. Notifications generally occur between the hours of 0500 and 2400 with the goal to conduct notification within the first 24-hour period following the incident; notification will be made as a matter of highest priority, taking precedence over all other responsibilities the notification officer may have. The Primary Next of Kin is notified first followed by Secondary Next of Kin.

Army Casualty Assistance Officer

Selection of Casualty Assistance Officers is made by a Soldier's chain of command. The Casualty Assistance Center which has responsibility for the geographical area in which the Primary Next of Kin or Person Authorized to Direct Disposition resides will appoint a Casualty Assistance Officer from trained and certified active duty personnel. The Casualty Assistance Officers will be knowledgeable, competent, dependable, sympathetic, and, if possible, able to communicate in the same language as the Primary Next of Kin or Person Authorized to Direct Disposition. Casualty Assistance Officers should meet the following qualifications:

(1) Mature Soldiers with six or more years of service.

(2) Officers in the rank of captain or higher, chief warrant officers in the rank of chief warrant officer two or higher, and noncommissioned officers in the rank of sergeant first class or higher.

(3) The grade of the Casualty Assistance Officer will, whenever possible, be equal to or higher than the grade of the casualty and equal to or higher than the grade of the Next of Kin when applicable.

Army Role of the Casualty Assistance Officer

Upon official notification of the Next of Kin, the Casualty Assistance Officer, as a minimum, will—

(1) Communicate directly with the person making the personal notification to help ensure the first and subsequent contacts with the Next of Kin are productive.

(2) Call the Next of Kin within four hours following initial notification to schedule an appointment to visit the Next of Kin. The Casualty Assistance Officer will determine the immediate needs or problems facing the Next of Kin and render prompt, courteous, and sympathetic assistance. The Casualty Assistance Officer, with the assistance of the supporting Casualty Assistance Center's Mortuary Affairs Specialist, will obtain the Person Authorized to Direct Disposition's decision on disposition of remains.

(3) Assist the Next of Kin in applying for all entitled benefits.

(4) Continue to support the Next of Kin until assistance is no longer required or the case is ready to transition to a case manager for long term management.

Army Extortion 17 Casualty Case Notes

On August 6, 2011, five Soldiers were Killed in Action in support of the Extortion 17 mission. Notification and assistance provided to the Soldiers' Next of Kin were completed in accordance with policy with two items of note:

(1) In one case, Secondary Next of Kin (parents) were notified prior to the Primary Next of Kin (spouse). Standard procedures for notification were followed, however the notification team was unable to establish contact with the Primary Next of Kin. As such, the team made contact with the Secondary Next of Kin for notification and followed up with the Primary Next of Kin with condolences and standard casualty support.

(2) In another case, it was identified that one of the Casualty Assistance Officers, who was properly trained on notification procedures, did not perform specific duties to the expected high level of standards when delivering such sensitive information to a Secondary Next of Kin (parent) under difficult circumstances. When this issue was identified, the Casualty Assistance Officer was relieved and immediately replaced to ensure the Next of Kin were as comfortable as possible throughout the assistance process. These notifications are difficult under the best of circumstances and even with training and guidance the task remains one that demands the highest emotional control and performance from the notifying officer.

Army Conclusion:

The circumstances surrounding the events of Extortion 17 are tragic. To lose even one precious life is one too many, and the United States Army lost five Soldiers that day. The Army recognizes that people are the Army, and our dedicated and talented force is the reason the United States Army is second to none. The Army remains committed to honor our Nation's commitment to the Soldiers and Families of deceased, injured, ill, and unaccounted-for through compassionate and responsive support.

Navy Casualty Overview

Navy families are, without doubt, an essential pillar of support to our operational readiness. When our uniformed men and women go in harm's way, they have leadership's unwavering commitment that the needs of their loved ones at home will be taken care of, particularly in a circumstance as tragic as a casualty. When a service member dies, is reported missing, captured, or is ill or injured, compassionate and timely care from our casualty assistance network is paramount in helping our families navigate the difficult road ahead.

Navy Casualty Assistance Process

The first priority of the casualty assistance program is to ensure the service member's immediate family is notified of the incident. This is followed by continuous information flow, as well as sustained assistance for as long as needed. To accomplish this, our three-tiered program consists of:

1) Casualty assistance staff at the Navy Personnel Command (NPC) in Millington, TN (herein referred to as "Navy Casualty")

2) Regional coordinators assigned to Commander, Navy Installations Command (CNIC) throughout the world

3) Approximately 6000 trained Casualty Assistance Calls Officers (CACOs) who personally assist the families.

Additionally, when a major crisis occurs the casualty enterprise is augmented by activation of NPC's Emergency Coordination Center, designed to respond to the significant volume of incoming phone calls that inevitably result from a casualty or disaster. The center is staffed by active duty personnel, 24/7, during an emergency to fill this vital requirement. Navy Casualty also has a reserve unit which specifically mobilizes to provide support during around-the-clock operations.

Casualty reporting, notification, and assistance requirements are outlined in Department of Defense Instruction (DODINST) 1300.18. Navy provides additional guidance in Commander, Navy Installations Command Instruction (CNICINST) 1770.2 and various Navy Military Personnel Manual (MILPERSMAN) articles. When a personnel casualty occurs, the member's commanding officer is required to submit a Personnel Casualty Report (PCR). This PCR is transmitted to all Casualty Assistance units: Navy Casualty (at Navy Personnel Command, in Millington, Tennessee) and each of the 24-hour Regional Operations Centers (ROCs). Navy Casualty verifies the information in the PCR against the Sailor's Official Military Personnel File, and the Regional coordinator assigns officer or senior enlisted CACOs to notify the next of kin. During notification, these CACOs may be accompanied by a Navy chaplain, if available.

Next of kin notifications routinely occur within 6-8 hours of receipt of the PCR; Primary NOK (PNOK) notification is considered the most urgent. Stipulations are in place stating timeliness may take precedence over procedure which enables someone from the command or the command's reporting senior to make initial notification. During this initial visit, the CACO, or notifying official, provides available releasable details concerning the death and renders immediate assistance to the family as the situation dictates.

Within one to two days of the casualty, the CACO arranges a second visit with the NOK to identify any immediate needs, arrange timely payment of the Death Gratuity (DG), and to discuss arrangements and entitlements associated with funeral or memorial services. At this visit, the CACO also discusses the options for interment (as outlined on the Statement of Disposition) with the Person Authorized to Direct Disposition (PADD) as designated on the Sailor's Record of Emergency Data (DD93).

In accordance with DoD policy, if a fatality occurs in a combat theater of operations, the deceased service member's remains are recovered and returned to the continental United States without delay. A Dignified Transfer of Remains (DTR) ceremony is performed upon arrival at Dover Air Force Base, Delaware. The PNOK, plus two additional family members, may travel at government expense to attend the DTR and the Secretary of the Navy may authorize additional family members to travel on a case-by-case basis.

The U.S. Navy has two active duty licensed morticians permanently assigned at Dover Air Force Base. During the DTR, these morticians meet with the PADD, the family, and if present, the CACO, to discuss mortuary affairs, options for funeral arrangements, and the DTR process. If the CACO and/or PADD do not accompany the PNOK to Dover, the Navy Mortician will brief the CACO, PADD, and funeral home via telephone after meeting with the family to discuss family concerns and other procedural issues. Once the DTR is complete and the family has departed Dover, the Navy and Armed Forces Medical Examiner (AFME) morticians begin the process of preparing and transporting the fallen Hero to his or her final resting place. This includes an AFME identification routine and autopsy, and a preparation of the Sailor's uniform by Navy morticians. AFME officials also provide a letter to the PADD and funeral home with specific details concerning the condition of the remains.

Approximately 10 working days after the member's death, the family receives a package from Navy Casualty discussing all remaining benefits and entitlements. The CACO will then schedule a third visit to assist the NOK in completing the remaining claims forms. The CACOs continue to assist all NOK as needed, until all benefits are paid or the family expressly states they no longer require further assistance. Upon completion of these duties, the CACO completes and submits to Navy Casualty a report indicating they have completed all duties and that all benefits have either been applied for or received.

Navy Actions for EXTORTION 17

Shortly after midnight on the morning of August 6, 2011, Navy Casualty began receiving phone calls concerning the possibility of a mass casualty – a CH-47 mishap in the Wardak Province of Afghanistan. Once the magnitude of the casualty became apparent – 22 Navy service members reported dead – standard protocol was initiated. Upon receipt of Personnel Casualty Reports indicating the deceased were assigned to Navy Special Warfare Development Group (NSWDG), NSWDG assigned CACO-trained personnel from their command to accomplish PNOK notifications and all follow-on casualty assistance. In accordance with the Navy's policy and procedures and based on records of the casualty teams, every family had a trained CACO, a notification official, a senior enlisted member, a cadre of administrative support provided by

NSWDG's Casualty Assistance and Calls Center (CAAC), and standardized regional and program manager level support.

In conjunction with Navy Casualty program managers and Regional CACOs, NSWDG representatives worked together consulting with the families on their remaining issues concerning benefits, entitlements, and travel pay as the cases progressed.

In closing, the Navy would like to emphasize the serious and sensitive approach we take towards our casualty assistance responsibilities. The Navy Casualty enterprise – from the Regions to the Program managers – is a community of professionals dedicated to the full spectrum of compassionate care for each and every family member. The Navy will continue to evaluate our programs to identify areas upon which we can improve – our Sailors and their families deserve nothing less.

Statement of

Mary Strange

Dear Senators, Congress and Members of The Armed Services Committee,

August 6,2011 was the most DEVASTING day in our lives. Every parent's WORST nightmare, your child has been killed, along with 30 of his comrades in a foreign country. Imagine...30 Families, who on 08/05/2011 were strangers, 24 hours later...bonded forever. My stepson, Michael Strange was on board the Chinook, call sign "EXTORTION 17", and in our home, the loud laughter isn't as loud and holidays, family get-togethers, celebrations and just any "ordinary" day, there is that silent void that NEVER goes away. I have had to watch my husband cry every single day because his heart aches and he misses his Son so much. Do you know what it's like, to watch the one person you love with ALL your heart, hurt sooo bad and know there's NOT A DAMN THING you can do?! I do, and it's a HORRIBLE feeling!

We have waited 30 months to be able to sit here today in the hope that this Committee would help us find out what REALLY happened that fateful night. Personally, I feel as if salt has been added to the wound by NOT ALLOWING any parents to speak here today. My husband & I have spent many sleepless nights, shed many tears and spent thousands of hours reading, researching, making calls and doing a whole lot of good ol' fashioned foot work knocking on doors trying to get some answers. In response we have been lied to, treated disrespectfully and talked to as if we were morons, it's disgraceful! I can't believe this is what Gold Star Parents have to tolerate!

There have been sooo many inconsistencies in the reports and stories for this to be "a lucky shot", so PLEASE DO NOT insult us with an OUTRAGEOUS AND OFFENSIVE excuse as that!!

Let's begin with Colt's statement in his "Summary" of what happened. He states that the "CH-47D Air Mission Commander and his task force commander **DETERMINED this mission to be BE A"HIGH-RISK MISSION" due to the experience level of one non-pilot crew chief** and because of this HIGH-RISK, the mission had to be approved by **The Higher Headquarters Commander for Special Operations Task Force** and the **Supporting Aviation Brigadier Commander".** W H O ARE THESE INCOMPETENT INDIVIDUALS? **W H Y WOULD THEY OK ALL 31 MEN ON 1 CH-47, IF BEFORE LEAVING THE FOB, IT WAS DETERMINED TO ALREADY BE A "HIGH RISK MISSION"?** T hen....
They Gave N O ESCORTS FOR "EXTORTION 17" ON an already "HIGH RISK MISSION" into a Hot Landing Zone (HLZ)? Standard Operating Procedures (SOP) Were Not Followed b/c they Should have had an escort (AC-130 Gunship OR an AH-64 Apache) upon leaving the FOB! **OUR MEN HAD NONE!**
Gen. Colt. states, "THE RANGER-led assault force was SUPPORTED by 2 CH-47D CHINOOK Helos and 2 AH-64 APACHE attack helicopters, along with an AC-130 Gunship, and a RELATIVELY ROBUST TEAM OF INTELLIGENCE, SURVEILLANCE AND RECONNAISSANCE (ISR) AIRCRAFT".
THEN to add insult to injury the next line is as follows "**THE 2 CH-47Ds WOULD AIRLIFT the Assault Force, totaling 47 personnel, into a LZ approx.. 1200 meters from the suspected location,** of the TANGI VALLEY TALIBAN LEADER, **QARI TAHIR** A.K.A- "**OBJECTIVE LEFTY GROVE".**

So there were 47 Rangers and 31 Americans aboard Extortion 17, that equals 78 of our Special Operators to CAPTURE 1 Taliban Leader??!! **W H Y??**

THEN...when the RANGERS arrived at their target compound, "Overhead Manned and Unmanned Aircraft" observed several personnel departing the target area. The AH-64 Apache attack helicopters **detected and Positively and Identified suspected TALIBAN FIGHTERS ARMED with AK-47 rifles and "RPG" LAUNCHERS, WALKING single file** APPROX. 400 meters **NORTHWEST** of the target compound." Throughout the execution of the mission the Overhead ISR aircraft continued to track the movement of suspected TALIBAN FIGHTERS". "THIS GROUP formed around two personnel who WERE OBSERVED MOVING **NORTHWEST** from the immediate vicinity of the target area, BEFORE the Ranger-led assault force had arrived". Did they know the Rangers were coming?...SURE SOUNDS LIKE THAT TO ME!!

"There were Taliban in the trees, on motorcycles, in the building, approx. 2 kilometers from the original compound". THEY KNEW ALL this, BUT STILL ALLOWED OUR "BOYS" to go IN A "HLZ", ALL 31 AMERICANS, ON ONE HELO???

** WE WERE TOLD THE RANGERS NEEDED HELP BECAUSE THEY WERE UNDER ATTACK......**

**THEN...WE COME TO FIND OUT...ARE YOU READY FOR THIS?...THE RANGERS WERE NEVER IN DANGER! **

*****OUR BOYS DID NOT HAVE TO BE DEPLOYED THAT NIGHT AS A IRF...SO...WHY WERE THEY???*****

The 7 Afghan Commandos who originally on "EXTORTION 17" either got off and refused to get back on OR were switched out and 7 New Afghans GOT ON.* **WHO were they?** WHY **were they NEVER questioned?** WHO made these decisions? HOW come General Colt **N E V E R** asks these questions? Are the 7 that aborted "EXTORTION 17" still being allowed to fly with our Special Operators? If so WHY?

*In the "Investigation Paperwork" "Ex. 89" Colt asks the Air Force Commander (AFC) "What is the assessment of the Tangi Valley?"   AFC answers "over 100 Taliban plan to travel from the ___ Province to the Tangi Valley to shoot down the Coalition Force Aircraft". They knew and did nothing to prevent this?!
WHY when our Men Requested Pre-Assault Fire 2-3 TIMES, to CLEAR THE HLZ... They were DENIED! WHO denied that request?

The Occupational Coordination Group (OCG) has the FINAL say in EVERY mission our Special Ops does, whether it is a go OR if they don't like it they can call the "mission" off!
HOW THE HELL CAN WE EVER WIN A WAR, WHEN THE ENEMY KNOWS ALL OUR MOVES BEFORE WE DO THEM?!

WHERE ARE THE "BLACK BOXES"? On Oct.12, 2011 General Colt, when my husband (Charles Strange) asks this question, Colt replies "A flash flood came and washed it away! We have looked into this and those Boxes DON'T go away, in fact they have BEACONS on them and can be found 20,000 ft UNDER WATER! SO we ask again...WHERE ARE THE "BLACK BOXES"? WHAT DON'T THEY WANT US TO HEAR ON THOSE RECORDINGS?

 There were 3 "EYES IN THE SKY"...BUT NOT 1 ON "EXTORTION 17"... WHY?
Gen. Colt asks about them and is told "We NEVER did a mission like this Sir (referring to Colt), it made us feel VERY Vulnerable. Our hands were tied from UP ABOVE"!
How far up is "UP ABOVE?" WHO gave this command? 95 days prior ALL EYES were on SEAL Team 6 from the SITUATION ROOM!

MY STEPSON, CTR1 MICHAEL STRANGE, WAS CREMATED...HE DID NOT NEED TO BE!
WHY WERE WE TOLD" *"THEY ARE ALL BURNED BEYOND RECOGNITION"*, *"NO IDENTIFIABLE REMAINS"* AND *"ONLY 38 C-SPINES AND SKULLS LEFT"*. LIES, LIES AND MORE LIES!!! WHY???

WE NEED HELP FINDING THE "TRUTH"

Why are the Parents and Loved Ones of "EXTORTION 17" BEING ALLOWED TO BE TREATED THIS WAY?

The Men of "EXTORTION 17" were Men of courage, integrity and honor, and not only did the Families lose their loved ones BUT this Country lost 30 Heroic Defenders of Freedom. PLEASE help the Families of Extortion 17 find some closure and that can only begin with the Truth. WE DESERVE THAT MUCH!

THE ONLY TIME YOU HAVE TO LIE... IS IF YOU KNOW WHAT YOU'RE DOING...IS WRONG!!

Statement of
J. Terry Pittman Gold star father Of S01 (SEAL) Jesse D. Pittman

GOD BLESS AMERICA

Initially we were one of three families that were asked to appear and talk. After much stress preparing for this, we were called and told that we weren't going to testify after all. I believe it was because of the lack of decorum which some of the families have shown. We were told that the Military were to talk instead. Normally I wouldn't have a problem with this, but unfortunately the Military brass answer to Politicians, and may have Political aspirations at some point in time.

I do feel some of the parents should be allowed to talk. Preferably in a closed hearing. I know a lot of conspiracy theories are running rampart, but I don't believe much of anything the most vocal are saying.

In my limited time I did some research on many of you. It has come to my attention that the majority of you are not Veterans and those that are have my deepest respect. (My point is that politics and our Great Nations Military are not in our country's best interest) I'm not saying we shouldn't have checks and balances, but let the Military determine how to fight the wars.

My family has the highest respect for our son, and the others aboard the helicopter. Our son and all the other men on the helicopter were very special people as all of you are aware. It is our hope that some good can come out of this and anything we can change to see that this doesn't happen again.

As a Vietnam Veteran, I didn't want our son to join the Military, not that I'm not unpatriotic, but for the fact when it comes to our children it is a different situation. Especially with our current rules of engagement, but I also didn't discourage him. Fortunately we were able to see him just before he deployed. He had just returned from another deployment and was back for a little over a month. My last words to him, (besides that I loved him) were: The two things that really concern me are the helicopters, and the Afghanis turning on them. His last words to me is "Don't worry Dad, I'll be home for Christmas"

This brings me to my questions: Why were the Afghanis switched out at the last minute? Who gave that order? It had to come from someone higher than the men in the field. Was Karzai in on the dispatch of our troops? Who from the State Department or CIA gave the go ahead for the mission? Where were the eyes in the sky? It is my understanding that DEVGRU only takes orders from someone in the administration.

If one of you should be elected President, what would be your exit strategy? What would you do more to protect our troops?

It is my hope we can win your hearts and minds. It is impossible to do this with our enemy. Since World War II, we haven't really won a war, North Korea, Vietnam, Iraq and now Afghanistan. Political correctness and our rules of engagement have to change. We are losing the finest people in the world to these asinine rules!

Mistakes were made and need to be corrected. Operation RED Wings rescue helicopter was also sent out without air support. We should have learned from that.

Nothing is ever going to bring our sons back. This is the most heart wrenching feeling we have ever experienced. There is not a day goes by when we don't think about him. To all of the other families including ones not on the helicopter who have lost a child they have our prayers and greatest sympathy

Let our Military win the wars. We have without a doubt the best Military in the world. Please quit tying their hands behind their backs.

Our soldiers should not be used for political gain. The administration should have kept their mouths shut when it comes to our missions and not disclosed who got Bin Laden. Poor example of leadership!!!

On closing, my wife brought up a good point. Counsel all the loved ones in a disaster like this. Parents, wives, and siblings. There were people left out.

Thank you for hearing me out.

To: House Oversight Committee Congressional Hearing
Thank you for your consideration
February 27. 2014 @ 10 a.m. EST
By Ida B. Pittman, Gold Star Mother
Jesse D. Pittman SEAL

FIRST THOUGHT

God Bless America is a prayer of many. Our country has been blessed by the mighty men of history. Many people of faith, came here for religious freedom, fought a mighty country for freedom and established a government that has lasted this long. Most of them confessed God as their sovereign leader. Our country, as a result, was blessed for many years. We became a world power, able to influence much in the positive that has gone on in the world to date. The wars we fought were not because we wanted a country's land or to control the people. Our history after a war has been to help to re-establish those countries.

In the last years the USA has turned away from the founding father's guidance. Religious guidance is synonymous with our moral integrity. Because of this lack of integrity, I believe God is taking His blessing away. As I understand, the chance of an RPG hitting the Chinook helicopter was a 1 in 500, this tells me God allowed this unfortunate tragedy. I know my son, who accepted Jesus Christ as his savior at age 13, is with the LORD. I know that several men on the helicopter were also saved. God took those *Mighty Men* home and left us to ponder the tragedy. I hope we grow from it personally and as a nation.

FIRST POINT

Our son was very concerned about his anonymity. We were asked not to use photos of him publicly. He did not have any social network accounts. We are certain he did other things to keep his security. We know the other team men did similar things. In fact, this attitude travels all the way down from WARCOM to the SEALs. So why are our people in public office not using the same degree of discretion? Why are our special operator's actions being announced to the public? Since this has become a common practice, what is being done to stop it? What discipline is being performed on those who do not use discretion? What is being done to edit our political representatives in the future?

SECOND POINT

After this tragedy we were overwhelmed and our heads were in a fog. Our family was devastated. As I have been connected with the other families, I know they were also. There were people like T.A.P.s reaching out to help us and we thank them immensely. We were given money to cover expenses and many useful things to read. Resources were many for us.

There was one area that we feel was forgotten and needs were not met.
Our other sons suffered as we, Jesse's parents did. As their mother, I grieved for them. I knew how hurt they were at the loss of their treasured brother.

My hope is that in the future, siblings need to be covered in the grief recovery programs. Again, siblings need to be better covered.

We want to thank everyone for all the help.

Everything in my mind has been turned upside down.

You are not supposed to bury your children. People frequently say, "Oh, I so am sorry I bought it up, but your son is a Hero." Well, let me tell all of those people who never buried a son or daughter. It does not matter if someone brings Michael's name up. It is not like you forget.

It comes whether you are driving, walking, in a store, or sleeping. It just comes. But, what we need to know is how to cope with this to go on for our other children or grandchildren. So, how do you do this when there is no closure? They tell us a "Lucky Shot"; they give us a book with no ink and no toner. I know the country is hurting, but come on! Then they have us come back 11 months later to bury the remains. All over again.
To cremate my son and then to find out he did not have to be cremated. What? ***Who? ***WHY***?

I will try and keep this short.
In the report, they saw the recording device [the Black Box] but there was a fire near the pilot. Then they say the flash flood washed the recording device away. They said a few times they thought they heard it? I would think they would know the different sounds. I am not military but I am pretty sure there is a unique sound.

Who came up with this mission? Why not the 160th? They are trained with a great deal of money spent on training 160th. That is who flies DEVGRU.
They did not have an alternate landing site? WHY NOT after the Rangers were there for 3 hours?

They knew how hot the area was from the previous mission. The previous mission was hit with everything yet they were not in a 1960 Chinook refurbished in 1985.They were in Black Hawks. They were told to abort the mission, but not Extortion-17 was NOT?
Where is SEAL Commander Van Hauser? We want him there.

Colt has multiple reports on the National Guard Unit from the day they went in until August 6, 2011. In fact, it's TOO much, as if he's TRYING to convince someone of something! He does that on OUR men BUT NOT on the Afghan Army? Not ONE WORD about the Afghan National Army. WHY? We don't even know who they were BECAUSE their names are NOT on the manifest. WHY don't they know who is with our MOST ELITE UNIT?

Colt says, and this is in the report too . . . are you ready for this? . . . "The

DRONES had A GLITCH IN THE Camera AND WERE NOT WORKING AT THE EXACT TIME OUR MEN WERE COMING IN." . . . REALLY?
And yet up until this point, there were NO PROBLEMS WITH THE CAMERAS OR THE DRONES!!! Do they expect us to believe this? Do they really think we are that stupid? Obviously THEY DO!!! And when we question them, they are such EGOMANIACS, they get ENRAGED!!! Also attacked by the NSA. [Phone and Computer]

They "piss in my face and tell me it is raining" . . . Really now?

Air force Commander tells Colt "we never did a mission like this, it made us feel very vulnerable" then he says "OUR HANDS WERE TIED FROM UP ABOVE". Who is the "up above"? HOW FAR "UP ABOVE" DOES THIS REACH?

While coming in a 50' tower on abuilding with 2 men up there in zero darkness? They called in to no other but to the "Afghan Administration" . . . of all people, and they told them "they were just hanging crops" . . . at 2 am? Who was the Afghan Administrator that night? WHO called the "Afghan Administration" to ask such a RIDICULOUS question??
At that "50 TOWER" APPROX. 30-40 Taliban were seen removing equipment out of there . . . what were they moving? Our Men found 6 IEDs placed around the "Tower"!

On the other side under the tree line there was 18 to 25 Taliban with AK-47's, motorcycles, RPGS, Night Vision Goggles (that worked), various machine guns, handguns, and cell phones.

After this "horse and pony show", General Colt received a promotion to Major General . . . WHAT? Just like the "Pat Tillman" case!
General Colt mentions the word "AMBUSH" a few times BUT DOES NOT follow up to investigate the answers he received . . . W H Y NOT???

Admiral McRaven, while at the "Aspen Security Forum" said in an interview with Wolf Blitzer "We rehearse every operation before we conduct it." If this is the case, then WHAT HAPPENED ON 8/6/11?
On August 24, 2012, McRaven also warned his troops both current and former "he would take LEGAL ACTION against ANYONE found to have exposed sensitive info that could cause fellow Forces harm". Associated PRESS 8-24-2012. **BUT DOES THAT INCLUDE JOE BIDEN & LEON PANETTA** for releasing the name of SEAL TEAM VI?? IF NOT . . . W H Y????

Army Aviation Regulation 95-1 states CH 47's can have as many as 3 different kinds of recorders such as:

a. (FDR) Flight Data Recorder
b. (CVR) Cock Pit Recorder
c. (DSC) Digital Source Collector
Someone by the call name of "S-3" was quoted "WE DID NOT have the full planning products". WHY NOT???

TV Sensor Operator-Two individuals are starting to brag over the internet and they actually said their names. They just killed SEAL Team 6. What are the names? How did they know who was in the Chinook?

Quair Tahir {AKA} objective Lefty Grove. If they are after him instead of the rescue mission for the Rangers, how did he know to move to another village? He KNEW him and his scumbag buddies. They knew. They Knew. They moved. The story went from rescue mission to going after Quair Tahir.
TF-Task Force is the first issue is to figure out what Helo went down. It took us 10 minutes to figure out what Helo went down. Coincidence my son, Michael jumped out of the Helo and few other people? Michael was intact except for his ankle and his hand was formed as though he was holding a gun. They did not know if anyone was alive but they did see a body cool down. WHAT the hell is going on? They don't know what Helo went down and then they watch my son DIE . . .

TM-J2*** The squirts {Taliban} leaders are back in Pakistan. They know when we are tracking them. You have to be out of your mind. They killed our sons and you know where they go in Pakistan and have TEA. It is in the paper work.

General Jeffery Colt asks what is the assessment of the Tangi Valley. AC says well sir on
May 10, 2011***One hundred Taliban are coming from ------- Providence to the Tangi Valley to shoot down the Coalition Force. They KNEW or is this just another coincidence?

General Colt asks what was the assessment for the rescue mission. After we found out what Helo went down which took them 10 minutes, we had 30 plans we had pathfinders, Black Hawks and 140 men. He said we waited for daylight because the area had so many Taliban. Who told them to wait? They could of saved my son, Michael. They said there was a big fireball, Michael was not burnt and some of the other men were not either. The clean up crew got there in a MH-47 S.O. Aircraft.

TF-CDR*** "SOP" They cannot go off, the FOB {Forward Operating Base} without an escort at night. {AWT} Who told them to go???

IO? This guy said J3 answerer's "Yes sir, there was a manifest" - and am sure you are aware of the 7 Afghan personnel that were not on the LIST but were on EXTORTION 17.

Colt asked "did we ever switch the sensor over the landing zone?" 1/B PLT CDR responds "Not to my knowledge." WHAT? Come on! ANOTHER Coincidence??

Aircraft Commander says really quickly an important point: We did pick up a few squirters and asked to fire and we were DENIED. {RULES OF ENGAGEMENT} And our sons get KILLED. {ROE}

Who was the contract crew and whom are they contracted from? What part did they play in the INFIL of Extortion 17? Did the contractor have anything to do with using only one ship?

Also what happened to Direct Support officer, a hobbit he has the capability to monitor push to talk?? We were not able to have DSO for that night? WHY 30 MEN and lets not use hobbit that night. ANOTHER Coincidence??

Also they say they heard the 3 minute-in call and one man said we have not heard anything from the guys . . . and then they heard the one minute call. THERE WAS A THIRTEEN-MINUTE LAPSE. Where is that TAPE????????? Coincidence? They lost that too.

We need the Armed Service Committee to stand up. WE NEED SOMEONE TO STAND UP TO THIS ESTABLISHMENT. We need to find out what really happened to our sons. God Bless the one million people who have shown their support.

I would personally like to thank Mr. Klayman & Ms. James for all their support.

Gold Star father of Michael Strange CTR1 KIA
8-6-2011   Extortion-17   DEVGRU

Mary & Charles Strange
215-983-4470

INTRODUCTION

I am Doug Hamburger. My wife, Shaune, and I are not confident that the official crash report – distributed to the families of Extortion 17 on October 12, 2011 – is complete and thus request answers to the inconsistencies contained in the redacted report. My son, SSG Patrick Douglas Hamburger was a full-time National Guard Army Aviation stationed out of Grand Island, Nebraska. Pat was the Flight Engineer and Gunner on the CH-47D Chinook that was shot down in what we feel may have been an ambush, on August 6th, 2011 with thirty (30) of America's finest troops.

We are very concerned that Vice President Biden and President Obama had disclosed on May 4th, 2011 that Navy SEAL Team VI had carried out a successful raid on Osama Bin Laden's compound resulting in the terrorist's death. Never before had a President in office released the identity of any Special Forces Team involved in a covert operation. Until Bin Laden was taken out, no one had really heard of SEAL Team VI. Its name and missions were always kept quiet for protection for themselves and their families.

Releasing their identity put a target on their backs, along with any support troops that went into battle with them, like the Army and Air Force Crew that were flying with them on the "Quick Reactionary Mission" when they were shot down.

Defense Secretary Robert Gates admitted that the SEAL Team that carried out the raid on Bin Laden now feared for their safety. Gates writes in his book, <u>Duty</u>, " . . . I had reminded everyone that the techniques, tactics, and procedures the SEALs had used in the Bin Laden operation were used every night in Afghanistan and elsewhere in hunting down terrorists and other enemies. It was therefore essential that we agree not to release any operational details of the raid. That we killed him, I said, is all we needed to say. That commitment lasted about five hours. The initial leaks came from the White House and CIA. They just couldn't wait to brag and to claim credit. The facts were often wrong, including details in the first press briefing. Nonetheless the information just kept pouring out. I was outraged and, at one point, told Donilson, 'Why doesn't everybody just shut the f*** up?' To no avail." Gates continues, "The SEALs shared with me their concerns about the leaks, particularly the fact that reporters were nosing around their communities trying to find them. They were worried about their families. I said we would do whatever was necessary to protect them . . ."

In a meeting with a group of Marines at Camp Lejeune in North Carolina, Robert Gates said, "we are very concerned about the security of our families, of your families and our troops, and also these elite units that are engaged in things like that. And without getting into details . . . I would tell you that when I met with the Team last Thursday, they expressed concern about that, and particularly with respect to their families." He then stated, "frankly, a week ago Sunday, in the Situation Room, we all agreed that we would not release any operational details from the effort to take out Bin Laden. That fell apart on Monday, the next day."

Gates said that the Department of Defense was looking into ways to "pump up the security" for the elite troops.

With Bounties on their heads and a target on their back, fifteen (15) Navy SEALs, seven (7) Navy Support, five (5) Army Aviation and three (3) Air Force Special Ops were shot down by the Taliban who were positioned in a tower of a building in the perfect place at the exact time to launch an attack on the CH-47D when it was most vulnerable – at landing.

How can anyone justify putting our troops at such risk?

SPECIFIC QUESTIONS

1. The investigation focused only on what happened but not why it happened. Who made the decision to not investigate those who were responsible for the loss of Extortion 17?
2. General Colt told Commanders that the Army's investigation into the downing of Extortion 17 was not to find fault. Why would the military conduct an investigation if it's main focus was not to find out all the facts surrounding the deaths of our sons?
3. Why were the seven (7) Afghans on the Chinook different than the ones listed on the manifest? Who was involved and who approved that decision? Did one of the Afghans compromise the mission? Was this another example of a green on blue attack?
4. It was the rules of engagement that dictated there had to be Afghans on that flight that night. Supposedly, we did not know if the group of men on the far side of town at 2:00 am were friendlies? Because there was a question if the "friendlies" were Taliban or not, Afghans had to be on the flight with our men. Common sense says that if they are moving away from the fighting to escape at that time of the night they were Taliban, not farmers who would have otherwise stayed in their homes.
5. In over 1250 pages of the investigation into the crash, why was the Afghan military not involved or even mentioned in the investigation? They were involved in all aspects of every mission. They had eight (8) men on the Chinook that night, including a civilian interpreter. It is hard to understand the omission. General Colt, who coordinated the investigation, should be investigated and we should find out who ultimately made the decision not to include the Afghan Command or any information they may have surrounding the crash. The pilot we talked with was in the initial meeting after the crash and the Afghan Command had records on each of our soldiers from the first day they joined the armed forces, including but not limited to their training and assignments up until the crash. With that type of thoroughness, how did they not investigate the Afghans?
6. Where is the black box? It must have a homing device. What was on it that the military said could not be found? Did something happen on the flight? It is highly unlikely that the black box was washed away in the flash flood if the

report is accurate regarding the recovering of the bodies. All bodies and body parts are said to have been found. The area had been "sanitized." Yet, with or without a homing device, the black box cannot be found?

7. Why did over thirteen (13) minutes pass between the 6-minute call and the one-minute call to land? Again, was there a fight on the Helicopter? Is this another example of a green on blue attack?

8. The request by the pilot for pre-assault fire was denied. The pre-assault fire would have been shot in a nearby area to draw the attention from the approach and landing site of the aircraft. No one likes to draw attention to where the aircraft is actually landing. (That may have been what the pilot was thinking that night knowing how narrow the valley was . . .) Why was it denied?

9. Why was the usual air support not stacked above the CH-47D as was customary on this type of mission? The two (2) CH-47Ds were the only aircraft on the mission. The other one was for secondary support. Thus, the other aircraft should have been support stacked above Extortion 17.

10. Why did the brigade not fully assess the dangers that Extortion 17 may encounter? My son Patrick told me for years that the #1 concern of any mission was to ensure the complete safety of the soldiers on that mission. All missions were well planned out with support stacked above the Chinooks to spot and attack the enemy and to ensure the safety of the crew on the Chinook.

11. Commanders had told General Colt's team that the Taliban had put one hundred (100) fighters in the Tangi Valley for the express purpose of bringing down a U.S. aircraft. This needs to be addressed.

12. How did the Taliban know to have men in a tower with RPGs in the landing zone where Extortion 17 would be flying? There had been no action any where near this spot all night.

13. Why was the decision made not to have the support stack positioned above Extortion 17? Protocol is to have two (2) Apaches, a C-130 Gunship and a drone stacked above the Chinook. The Apaches were to fly in low enough with the Chinook to escort it to the landing spot. The Apaches were looking for squirters instead of searching for enemies that would attack Extortion 17. The C-130 had its eyes on the landing spot. Supposedly, the drone's eye in the sky was not working. No one was looking out for the safety of the crew on this Special Ops mission. Why was protocol not followed? Why was their safety compromised? Those aircrafts should have been ordered to follow protocol before Extortion 17 entered the valley.

14. Why didn't the two (2) Apaches inspect the landing zone, as was protocol until three (3) minutes before Extortion 17 was to land? There were two (2) people in the landing zone. Protocol would have had the landing called off with two (2) people running around the landing zone. The Apaches did not arrive in time to call off the landing.

15. Why did the Special Operations Commander at headquarters not order the two (2) Apaches to inspect the landing site? The last-second-order was given

by a Ranger Commander on the ground. Who was the SOC? Was he Afghan or NATO?

16. Protocol on mission planning was to have a primary landing zone and an alternative landing zone. During the mission planning, an alternative-landing zone was not assigned. Why was that?

17. Why were there at least five (5) heavily armed enemy 800 meters to the east of the landing zone? Did they know our sons would be landing there? How did they know to go there? Who tipped them off? Especially when – in the crash report – it mentions men on the ground with radios.

18. Why were the approach and the landing zone not properly vetted or guarded?

19. General Colt said the drone over the CH-47D had a glitch and the camera was off. We had two (2) soldiers report that they had watched Extortion 17 get shot down from two (2) separate FOBs. We request a copy of that shoot down, to have an expert look at it and tell us what he thinks may have happened. Why were we lied to about the camera being turned off?

20. Why was a CH-47D used in this mission? The mission was in a valley at a hot landing zone, flying in through a narrow entrance with buildings on each side. Two previous missions with CH-47D's that tried to land in that valley had to abort because of enemy fire. With that previous history, why wasn't the MH-47 used? They were used immediately to pick up the Army Rangers and to bring troops to the crash site.

21. Billy Vaughn and Charlie Strange both mentioned that Captain Van Houser, who was SEAL Team Commander at the time, is no longer in command and has not been heard from since. What happened to him? Why did he disappear? What does he know about that night?

22. Why was there no mention of the other two (2) Apaches that crashed that night? One crashed trying to climb the valley walls instead of flying out of the valley, through the entrance where Extortion 17 was shot down.

23. There were a large number of increased missions in the years leading up to Extortion 17. The 82nd Brigade was constantly bragging about how many more missions they were doing than the 10th Mountain that was pulled out earlier. Why was there so much focus on how many missions were being done? Did it compromise the safety of our troops?

24. Who made the decision to send an IRF after a group of squirters? An ARF is sent in to rescue our men when they are in trouble. An IRF is a pre-planned base contingency developed during the initial briefing before a mission. It is planned to counteract an enemy's possible movement. Extortion 17 was sent in as an IRF. Using them in this manner was not protocol. How could a change like this come out of a 50-minute meeting, three (3) hours into a mission? Who suggested this change in protocol? Who influenced this change? Who approved it?

25. Why was Extortion 17 sent on a mission at all? There was no significant intelligence. In Colt's report he asked, "how often did a mission like this take place?" Never! No one questioned, had any knowledge of a mission that was sent to catch squirters. Special Forces had never been sent on a mission like

this. Who came up with this mission? Was it the Afghan Command?

26. How could Extortion 17's mission be off the ground before the Brigade's top Officer was made aware of the mission? How could this happen, especially when Special Ops were involved?

27. Thirty (30) minutes after Extortion 17 was shot down, the Taliban bragged on the Internet that they had shot down SEAL Team VI in a helicopter. How did they know members of SEAL Team VI were on that Chinook unless they were tipped off?

RAMP CEREMONY

At the Ramp Ceremony in Kabul, a Muslim Imam was allowed to say a prayer over the caskets bearing the bodies of our sons. Apparently, no one vetted what he was going to say. In Arabic, he disparaged the memories of our sons, damning them as infidels to Allah. The Imam said they are burning in hell, while the Muslims who were with them are in heaven. Yet, our military prohibited any mention of a Judeo-Christian God at the ceremony. Families are usually given a copy of the Ramp Ceremony honoring their loved one. None of the Families of Extortion 17 were given a copy. Someone made the decision to cover up how our son's were degraded and humiliated in a ceremony that was meant to honor them for the sacrifice they had made for our country. Who allowed the Imam to speak? Who decided to cover it up? Why has no one has ever apologized to the families for ever letting something so disrespectful to happen?

RULES OF ENGAGEMENT

The United States has the greatest military in the world. Our troops have the best training, the best weaponry and the best military minds.

When our military is training, one of its top concerns is safety – the safety of the men they are fighting with as well as their own safety.

The Rules of Engagement in the Middle East limit our forces from fighting to the best of their abilities. They also expose our forces to unnecessary risks, compromising their safety.

The Rules of Engagement should be created to protect our troops, not to protect a population that chooses to hide and protect our enemy.

It was because of the Rules of Engagement that seven (7) Afghan commandoes were onboard Extortion 17. If it is not known for sure that the people we are after are the enemy, we need to bring Afghans and an interpreter. Because those seven (7) were switched with Afghans that were not properly vetted out less than thirty (30) minutes before the mission, they could have compromised the mission, as would be consistent with the increase of green on blue attacks.

We could not fire on the turret where the two (2) men who shot down Extortion 17 were located, because of the Rules of Engagement. It was not known if any innocent people were inside the building. The Taliban can use a building to attack us, but we cannot shoot at them.

Helicopters returning to base see the enemy setting up rockets aimed at the military base, but cannot fire at them unless they fire first.

The requested pre-assault fire as the Chinook entered the valley was denied because the rules of engagement would not allow the fire unless we could be certain no one would be hurt.

Our troops cannot fire at someone, unless they are shot at first. Even if they see a gun or a weapon, they cannot shoot.

The Rules of Engagement require so many Afghans to be on certain missions. Some missions are canceled because not enough Afghans show up for the mission to take place.

CONCLUSION

From what we have learned thus far in our correspondence with congressional staff, the military seeks to explain in *their* way these unanswered questions by claiming " . . . this is just a series of unfortunate events." If it were only a question of one or two "events", then perhaps there would be some plausibility to this. But, when there are thirty and more unanswered questions, and when there is no concerted effort to get to the bottom of this by our Commander in Chief and his military brass, one can only conclude that the circumstances surrounding the death of my son and his colleagues are being covered up. This regrettable conclusion is heightened by the decision of this Sub-Committee and Committee to bar any of the family members to give live testimony at the hearing to be held on February 27, 2014.

Never before in this history of our country have we seen such a callous disregard for the well-being of the nation's best and brightest fighting men who gave their lives without reservation in a poorly conceived war that the nation has essentially already lost.

As a father, what am I to think and feel when those who have the capacity to expose what truly happened hide their heads in the sand for cover? For the rest of my life, my loss will only grow greater knowing that when I asked for help to those responsible in Government, little has been forthcoming.

I thank the Committee for holding this hearing and I pray that it is able to shed light upon some of these questions.

RECORD OF EMERGENCY DATA

PRIVACY ACT STATEMENT

AUTHORITY: 5 USC 552, 10 USC 655, 1475 to 1480 and 2771, 38 USC 1970, 44 USC 3101, and EO 9397 (SSN).
PRINCIPAL PURPOSES: This form is used by military personnel and Department of Defense civilian and contractor personnel, collectively referred to as civilians, when applicable. **For military personnel,** it is used to designate beneficiaries for certain benefits in the event of the Service member's death. It is also a guide for disposition of that member's pay and allowances if captured, missing or interned. It also shows names and addresses of the person(s) the Service member desires to be notified in case of emergency or death. **For civilian personnel,** it is used to expedite the notification process in the event of an emergency and/or the death of the member. The purpose of soliciting the SSN is to provide positive identification. All items may not be applicable.
ROUTINE USES: None.
DISCLOSURE: Voluntary; however, failure to provide accurate personal identifier information and other solicited information will delay notification and the processing of benefits to designated beneficiaries if applicable.

INSTRUCTIONS TO SERVICE MEMBER	INSTRUCTIONS TO CIVILIANS
This extremely important form is to be used by you to show the names and addresses of your spouse, children, parents, and any other person(s) you would like notified if you become a casualty (other family members or fiance), and, to designate beneficiaries for certain benefits if you die. IT IS YOUR RESPONSIBILITY to keep your Record of Emergency Data up to date to show your desires as to beneficiaries to receive certain death payments, and to show changes in your family or other personnel listed, for example, as a result of marriage, civil court action, death, or address change.	This extremely important form is to be used by you to show the names and addresses of your spouse, children, parents, and any other person(s) you would like notified if you become a casualty. Not every item on this form is applicable to you. **This form is used by the Department of Defense (DoD) to expedite notification in the case of emergencies or death.** It does not have a legal impact on other forms you may have completed with the DoD or your employer.

IMPORTANT: This form is divided into two sections: Section 1 - Emergency Contact Information and Section 2 - Benefits Related Information. READ THE INSTRUCTIONS ON PAGES 3 AND 4 BEFORE COMPLETING THIS FORM.

SECTION 1 - EMERGENCY CONTACT INFORMATION

1. NAME (Last, First, Middle Initial)	2. SSN

3a. SERVICE/CIVILIAN CATEGORY	b. REPORTING UNIT CODE/DUTY STATION
☐ ARMY ☐ NAVY ☐ MARINE CORPS ☐ AIR FORCE ☐ DoD ☐ CIVILIAN ☐ CONTRACTOR	

4a. SPOUSE NAME (If applicable) (Last, First, Middle Initial)	b. ADDRESS (include ZIP Code) AND TELEPHONE NUMBER
☐ SINGLE ☐ DIVORCED ☐ WIDOWED	

5. CHILDREN a. NAME (Last, First, Middle Initial)	b. RELATIONSHIP	c. DATE OF BIRTH (YYYYMMDD)	d. ADDRESS (include ZIP Code) AND TELEPHONE NUMBER

6a. FATHER NAME (Last, First, Middle Initial)	b. ADDRESS (Include ZIP Code) AND TELEPHONE NUMBER

7a. MOTHER NAME (Last, First, Middle Initial)	b. ADDRESS (Include ZIP Code) AND TELEPHONE NUMBER

8a. DO NOT NOTIFY DUE TO ILL HEALTH	b. NOTIFY INSTEAD

9a. DESIGNATED PERSON(S) (Military only)	b. ADDRESS (Include ZIP Code) AND TELEPHONE NUMBER

10. CONTRACTING AGENCY AND TELEPHONE NUMBER (Contractors only)

DD FORM 93, JAN 2008 PREVIOUS EDITION IS OBSOLETE. Adobe 7.0 Professional

SECTION 2 - BENEFITS RELATED INFORMATION			
11a. BENEFICIARY(IES) FOR DEATH GRATUITY *(Military only)*	b. RELATIONSHIP	c. ADDRESS *(Include ZIP Code)* AND TELEPHONE NUMBER	d. PERCENTAGE
12a. BENEFICIARY(IES) FOR UNPAID PAY/ALLOWANCES *(Military only)* **NAME AND RELATIONSHIP**		b. ADDRESS *(Include ZIP Code)* AND TELEPHONE NUMBER	c. PERCENTAGE
13a. PERSON AUTHORIZED TO DIRECT DISPOSITION (PADD) *(Military only)* **NAME AND RELATIONSHIP**		b. ADDRESS *(Include ZIP Code)* AND TELEPHONE NUMBER	

14. CONTINUATION/REMARKS

15. SIGNATURE OF SERVICE MEMBER/CIVILIAN *(Include rank, rate, or grade if applicable)*	16. SIGNATURE OF WITNESS *(Include rank, rate, or grade as appropriate)*	17. DATE SIGNED *(YYYYMMDD)*

DD FORM 93 (BACK), JAN 2008

81

INSTRUCTIONS FOR PREPARING DD FORM 93

(See appropriate Service Directives for supplemental instructions for completion of this form at other than MEPS)

All entries explained below are for electronic or typewriter completion, except those specifically noted. If a computer or typewriter is not available, print in black or blue-black ink insuring a legible image on all copies. Include "Jr.," "Sr.," "III" or similar designation for each name, if applicable. When an address is entered, include the appropriate ZIP Code. If the member cannot provide a current address, indicate "unknown" in the appropriate item. Addresses shown as P.O. Box Numbers or RFD numbers should indicate in Item 14, "Continuations/Remarks", a street address or general guidance to reach the place of residence. In addition, the notation "See Item 14" should be included in the item pertaining to the particular next of kin or when the space for a particular item is insufficient. If the address for the person in the item has been shown in a preceding item, it is unnecessary to repeat the address; however, the name must be entered. Those items that are considered not applicable to civilians will be left blank.

ITEM 1. Enter full last name, first name, and middle initial.

ITEM 2. Enter social security number (SSN).

ITEM 3a. Service. **Military:** Mark X in appropriate block. **Civilian:** Mark two blocks as appropriate. Examples: an Army civilian would mark Army and either Civilian or Contractor; a DoD civilian, without affiliation to one of the Military Services, would mark DoD and then either Civilian or Contractor as appropriate.

ITEM 3b. Reporting Unit Code/Duty Station. See Service Directives.

ITEM 4a. Spouse Name. Enter last name (if different from Item 1), first name and middle initial on the line provided. If single, divorced, or widowed, mark appropriate block.

ITEM 4b. Address and Telephone Number. Enter the "actual" address and telephone number, not the mailing address. Include civilian title or military rank and service if applicable. If one of the blocks in 4a is marked, leave blank.

ITEM 5a-d. Children. Enter last name (only if different from Item 1) first name and middle initial, relationship, and date of birth of all children. If none, so state. Include illegitimate children if acknowledged by member or paternity/maternity has been judicially decreed. Relationship examples: son, daughter, stepson or daughter, adopted son or daughter or ward. Date of birth example: 19950704. For children not living with the member's current spouse, include address and name and relationship of person with whom residing in item 5d.

ITEM 6a. Father Name. Last name, first name and middle initial.

ITEM 6b. Address and Telephone Number of Father. If unknown or deceased, so state. Include civilian title or military rank and service if applicable. If other than natural father is listed, indicate relationship.

ITEM 7a. Mother Name. Last name, first name and middle initial.

ITEM 7b. Address and Telephone Number of Mother. If unknown or deceased, so state. Include civilian title or military rank and service if applicable. If other than natural mother is listed, indicate relationship.

ITEM 8. Persons Not to be Notified Due to Ill Health.
a. List relationship, e.g., "Mother," of person(s) listed in Items 4, 5, 6, or 7 who are not to be notified of a casualty due to ill health. If more than one child, specify, e.g., "daughter Susan." Otherwise, enter "None".
b. List relationship, e.g., "Father" or name and address of person(s) to be notified in lieu of person(s) listed in item 8a. If "None" is entered in Item 8a, leave blank.

ITEM 9a. This item will be used to record the name of the person or persons, if any, other than the member's primary next of kin or immediate family, to whom information on the whereabouts and status of the member shall be provided if the member is placed in a missing status. Reference 10 USC, Section 655. **NOT APPLICABLE to civilians.**

ITEM 9b. Address and telephone number of Designated Person(s). **NOT APPLICABLE to civilians.**

ITEM 10. Contracting Agency and Telephone Number **(Contractors only). NOT APPLICABLE to military personnel.** Civilian contractors will provide the name of their contracting agency and its telephone number. Example: XYZ Electric, (703) 555-5689. The telephone number should be to the company or corporation's personnel or human resources office.

ITEM 11a. Beneficiary(ies) for Death Gratuity **(Military only)**. Enter first name(s), middle initial, and last name(s) of the person(s) to receive death gratuity pay. A member may designate one or more persons to receive all or a portion of the death gratuity pay. The designation of a person to receive a portion of the amount shall indicate the percentage of the amount, to be specified only in 10 percent increments, that the person may receive. If the member does not wish to designate a beneficiary for the payment of death gratuity, enter "None," or if the full amount is not designated, the payment or balance will be paid as follows:

(1) To the surviving spouse of the person, if any;
(2) To any surviving children of the person and the descendants of any deceased children by representation;
(3) To the surviving parents or the survivor of them;
(4) To the duly appointed executor or administrator of the estate of the person;
(5) If there are none of the above, to other next of kin of the person entitled under the laws of domicile of the person at the time of the person's death.

The member should make specific designations, as it expedites payment.

DD FORM 93 (INSTRUCTIONS), JAN 2008

INSTRUCTIONS FOR PREPARING DD FORM 93
(Continued)

ITEM 11a. *(Continued)* Seek legal advice if naming a minor child as a beneficiary. If a member has a spouse but designates a person other than the spouse to receive all or a portion of the death gratuity pay, the Service concerned is required to provide notice of the designation to the spouse. **NOT APPLICABLE to civilians.**

Item 11b. Relationship. **NOT APPLICABLE to civilians.**

ITEM 11c. Enter beneficiary(ies) full mailing address and telephone number to include the ZIP Code. **NOT APPLICABLE to civilians.**

ITEM 11d. Show the percentage to be paid to each person. Enter 10%, 20%, 30%, up to 100% as appropriate. The sum shares must equal 100 percent. If no percent is indicated and more than one person is named, the money is paid in equal shares to the persons named. **NOT APPLICABLE to civilians.**

ITEM 12a. Beneficiary(ies) for Unpaid Pay/Allowance **(Military only)**. Enter first name(s), middle initial, last name(s) and relationship of person to receive unpaid pay and allowances at the time of death. The member may indicate anyone to receive this payment. If the member designated two or more beneficiaries, state the percentage to be paid each in item 10c. If the member does not wish to designate a beneficiary, enter "By Law." The member is urged to designate a beneficiary for unpaid pay and allowances as payment will be made to the person in order of precedence by law (10 USC 2771) in the absence of a designation. Seek legal advice if naming a minor child as beneficiary. **NOT APPLICABLE to civilians.**

ITEM 12b. Enter beneficiary(ies) full mailing address and telephone number to include the ZIP Code. **NOT APPLICABLE to civilians.**

ITEM 12c. If the member designated two or more beneficiaries, state the percentage to be paid each in this section. The sum shares must equal 100 percent. **NOT APPLICABLE to civilians.**

ITEM 13a. Enter the name and relationship of the Person Authorized to Direct Disposition (PADD) of your remains should you become a casualty. Only the following persons may be named as a PADD: surviving spouse, blood relative of legal age, or adoptive relatives of the decedent. If neither of these three can be found, a person standing in loco parentis may be named. **NOT APPLICABLE to civilians.**

ITEM 13b. Address and telephone number of PADD. **NOT APPLICABLE to civilians.**

ITEM 14. Continuations/Remarks. Use this item for remarks or continuation of other items, if necessary. Prefix entry with the number of the item being continued; for example, 5/John J./son/ 19851220/321 Pecan Drive, Schertz TX 78151. Also use this item to list name, address, and relationship of other persons the member desires to be notified. Other dependents may also be listed. This block offers the greatest amount of flexibility for the member to record other important information not otherwise requested but considered extremely useful in the casualty notification and assistance process. Besides continuing information from other blocks on this form, the member may desire to include additional information such as: NOK language barriers, location or existence of a Will, additional private insurance information, other family member contact numbers, etc. If additional space is required, attach a supplemental sheet of standard bond paper with the information.

ITEM 15. Signature of Service Member/Civilian. Check and verify all entries and sign all copies in ink as follows: First name, middle initial, last name. Include rank, rate, or grade if applicable. May be electronically signed (see DoD Instruction 1300.18 for guidelines).

ITEM 16. Signature of Witness. Have a witness (disinterested person) sign all copies in ink as follows: First name, middle initial, last name. Include rank, rate, or grade as appropriate. A witness signature is not required for electronic versions of the DD Form 93 (see DoD Instruction 1300.18).

ITEM 17. Date the member or civilian signs the form. This item is an ink entry and must be completed on all copies.

U.S. DEPARTMENT OF DEFENSE

Search

| HOME | TODAY IN DOD | ABOUT DOD | TOP ISSUES | NEWS | PHOTOS/VIDEOS | MILITARY/DOD WEBSITES | CONTACT US |

News
- DOD News Page
- News Articles
- News/Casualty Releases
- Press Advisories
- News Transcripts
- Publications
- Speeches
- Contracts
- Testimony
- Messages
- Special Reports

Secretary of Defense
- Biography
- Speeches
- Messages
- Testimony
- Travels
- News Photos

Deputy Secretary of Defense
- Biography
- Speeches
- Travels
- News Photos

Photos/Videos
- Lead Photos
- News Photos
- Photo Essays
- Week in Photos
- Videos
- Pentagon Channel
- Imagery Archive

Other
- Briefing Slides
- Pentagon Press Passes
- Press/Media Queries
- Military Commissions
- Detainee
- Other News Sources

News Release

Press Operations

SHARE

NEWS RELEASE   E-MAIL A COPY | PRINTER FRIENDLY | LATEST NEWS RELEASES

IMMEDIATE RELEASE

Release No: 705-11
August 11, 2011

DOD Identifies Service Members Killed in CH-47 Crash

The Department of Defense announced today the deaths of 30 servicemembers who were supporting Operation Enduring Freedom. They died Aug. 6 in Wardak province, Afghanistan, of wounds suffered when their CH-47 Chinook helicopter crashed.

The following sailors assigned to an East Coast-based Naval Special Warfare unit were killed:

Lt. Cmdr. (SEAL) Jonas B. Kelsall, 32, of Shreveport, La.,

Special Warfare Operator Master Chief Petty Officer (SEAL) Louis J. Langlais, 44, of Santa Barbara, Calif.,

Special Warfare Operator Senior Chief Petty Officer (SEAL) Thomas A. Ratzlaff, 34, of Green Forest, Ark.,

Explosive Ordnance Disposal Technician Senior Chief Petty Officer (Expeditionary Warfare Specialist/Freefall Parachutist) Kraig M. Vickers 36, of Kokomo, Hawaii,

Special Warfare Operator Chief Petty Officer (SEAL) Brian R. Bill, 31, of Stamford, Conn.,

Special Warfare Operator Chief Petty Officer (SEAL) John W. Faas, 31, of Minneapolis, Minn.,

Special Warfare Operator Chief Petty Officer (SEAL) Kevin A. Houston, 35, of West Hyannisport, Mass.,

Special Warfare Operator Chief Petty Officer (SEAL) Matthew D. Mason, 37, of Kansas City, Mo.,

Special Warfare Operator Chief Petty Officer (SEAL) Stephen M. Mills, 35, of Fort Worth, Texas,

Explosive Ordnance Disposal Technician Chief Petty Officer (Expeditionary Warfare Specialist/Freefall Parachutist/Diver) Nicholas H. Null, 30, of Washington, W.Va.,

Special Warfare Operator Chief Petty Officer (SEAL) Robert J. Reeves, 32, of Shreveport, La.,

Special Warfare Operator Chief Petty Officer (SEAL) Heath M. Robinson, 34, of Detroit, Mich.,

Special Warfare Operator Petty Officer 1st Class (SEAL) Darrik C. Benson, 28, of Angwin, Calif.

Special Warfare Operator Petty Officer 1st Class (SEAL/Parachutist) Christopher G. Campbell, 36, of Jacksonville, N.C.,

Information Systems Technician Petty Officer 1st Class (Expeditionary Warfare Specialist/Freefall Parachutist) Jared W. Day, 28, of Taylorsville, Utah,

Master-at-Arms Petty Officer 1st Class (Expeditionary Warfare Specialist) John Douangdara, 26, of South Sioux City, Neb.,

Cryptologist Technician (Collection) Petty Officer 1st Class (Expeditionary Warfare Specialist) Michael J. Strange, 25, of Philadelphia, Pa.,

Special Warfare Operator Petty Officer 1st Class (SEAL/Enlisted Surface Warfare Specialist) Jon T. Tumilson, 35, of Rockford, Iowa,

Special Warfare Operator Petty Officer 1st Class (SEAL) Aaron C. Vaughn, 30, of Stuart, Fla., and

Special Warfare Operator Petty Officer 1st Class (SEAL) Jason R. Workman, 32, of Blanding, Utah.

The following sailors assigned to a West Coast-based Naval Special Warfare unit were killed:

Special Warfare Operator Petty Officer 1st Class (SEAL) Jesse D. Pittman, 27, of Ukiah, Calif., and

Special Warfare Operator Petty Officer 2nd Class (SEAL) Nicholas P. Spehar, 24, of Saint Paul, Minn.

The soldiers killed were:

Chief Warrant Officer David R. Carter, 47, of Centennial, Colo. He was assigned to the 2nd Battalion, 135th Aviation Regiment (General Support Aviation Battalion), Aurora, Colo.;

Chief Warrant Officer Bryan J. Nichols, 31, of Hays, Kan. He was assigned to the 7th Battalion,

http://www.defense.gov/releases/release.aspx?releaseid=14728

Most Recent News Releases

04/02/2014
Statement from Secretary of Defense Hagel on Fort Hood

04/02/2014
DoD Identifies Army Casualty

04/02/2014
Navy to Commission Littoral Combat Ship Coronado

04/01/2014
Flag Officer Announcements

04/01/2014
General Officer Announcement

04/01/2014
General Officer Assignments

04/01/2014
Secretary of Defense and Chairman of the Joint Chiefs of Staff issue Video Message on Sexual Assault Awareness Month

03/31/2014
Readout of Secretary of Defense Chuck Hagel's Meeting with Portuguese Minister of Defense Pedro Aguiar-Branco

03/31/2014
General Officer Assignments

03/28/2014
Senior Executive Service Announcement

84

158th Aviation Regiment (General Support Aviation Battalion), New Century, Kan.;

Staff Sgt. Patrick D. Hamburger, 30, of Lincoln, Neb. He was assigned to the 2nd Battalion, 135th Aviation Regiment (General Support Aviation Battalion), Grand Island, Neb.;

Sgt. Alexander J. Bennett, 24, of Tacoma, Wash. He was assigned to the 7th Battalion, 158th Aviation Regiment (General Support Aviation Battalion), New Century, Kan.; and

Spc. Spencer C. Duncan, 21, of Olathe, Kan. He was assigned to the 7th Battalion, 158th Aviation Regiment (General Support Aviation Battalion), New Century, Kan.

The airmen killed were:

Tech. Sgt. John W. Brown, 33, of Tallahassee, Fla.;

Staff Sgt. Andrew W. Harvell, 26, of Long Beach, Calif.; and

Tech. Sgt. Daniel L. Zerbe, 28, of York, Pa.

All three airmen were assigned to the 24th Special Tactics Squadron, Pope Field, N.C.

For more information about the sailors, media may contact Lt. Arlo Abrahamson at 757-763-2007 or 757-620-3109.

For more information on Carter, media may contact the Colorado National Guard public affairs office at 720-250-1053.

For more information on Nichols, Bennett and Duncan, media may contact the 11th Aviation Command public affairs office at 502-626-5746 or 502-651-3466.

For more information on Hamburger, media may contact the Nebraska National Guard public affairs office at 402-309-7302 or 402-309-7303.

For more information about the airmen, media may contact the Air Force Special Operations Command public affairs office at 850-884-5515.

UPDATE: August 12, 2011 -- Sgt. Hamburger was posthumously promoted to staff sergeant.

Home	Inspector General	Join the Military
Today in DOD	Privacy & Security	Careers
About DOD	Link Disclaimer	Web Policy
Top Issues	Recovery Act	
News	FOIA	
Photos/Videos	USA.gov	
Military/DoD Websites	No FEAR Act	
Contact Us	Plain Writing Act of 2010	
	Accessibility/Section 508	

STAY CONNECTED

RSS Feeds   Email   Widgets   DOD Live Blog   Facebook   Twitter

YouTube   Flickr

MORE SOCIAL MEDIA SITES »